THE GREAT BOOK
OF COUNTRY MUSIC

Amazing Trivia, Fun Facts &
The History of Country Music

Bill O'Neill

ISBN: 978-1-64845-071-6

DON'T FORGET YOUR
FREE BOOKS

CONTENTS

INTRODUCTION

There is a reason why the history of country music cannot be told chronologically. It is much like the history of America itself. Different things happened at different places at the same time, and the overall result from those events is even more diversity, rather than convergence. In a way, this is both the beauty and the tragedy of country music.

Who makes and who listens to country music anyway? Technically speaking, every kid nowadays who grabs a guitar and strums the 'G' chord plays country. This genre is so deeply rooted into all modern music that it is impossible to isolate it and say, "Here—this is country." That would be like extracting the eggs from a cooked cake.

How did it all start? Was there one single musician who made the first country record? Yes, there was, as you will see. But that musician drew his inspiration and material from a long tradition of rural mountain folk. Nobody knows the origins of most classic country songs—such as "Man of Constant Sorrow." But what we do know is that country came down from the rural southern mountains and has been making its way into every American's life for generations.

Those who chanted old country songs up in the mountain shacks and churches were the generation before the big city and economic power. They were rural workers, who lived simple and honest lives and believed in God from the bottom of their hearts. Because they really needed him.

So, when someone speaks of the origins of country music, they shouldn't start with a single record or artists. Real country music, just like real gospel music, has no author, no commercial intent, and no pretense. We are getting farther and farther from those Victorian morals and ideals, yet every new generation seeks more and more of that indescribable authenticity of faith, sorrow, and hope. And the deeper we dig, the more lost we get.

Driving alone on a lost highway; this is as close as we can get to country music today. And it feels good. But it feels even better to know the history of that genre—to know about the streams that filled this restless river through the years. Whether you realize it or not, you—as an American or country music fan—are also a part of that history.

On the other hand, everyone wants to be the best at trivia games and quizzes. And country music is an advanced topic, isn't it? Well, not anymore—we hope. We wrote this book in a way that gives you the right knowledge and skips the part where you get overloaded with information and fall asleep.

Also, knowing the history of country music is not just about facts and dates. It's about understanding and connecting the dots between all those events and people who have shaped up and maintained the genre. The best way to reach this goal is, of course, to have fun along the way. And this is what we've tried to achieve here.

We wish you a pleasant journey from the deep mountains to the mega polis, all along an endless dusty highway. Do not focus on the wiggly chronological sequences. Rather, try to accept the beauty of infinity. And maybe that whole journey will change your perception of not only country music, but also the vast country that you live in.

CHAPTER 1

THE CARTERS COME DOWN
FROM THE MOUNTAINS.

The birthplace of country music is said to be the Appalachian Mountains. In the 18th century, the small mountain villages there were populated by settlers from Britain and Ireland, who usually spent their whole lives working and producing food to sustain themselves.

The church was a hugely important institution in these mountain villages. Church buildings had to be maintained and kept clean because they were the spots where people would gather after a working day and at the end of the week. It was during maintenance time that the first country tunes were whistled.

At gatherings, people gradually started singing these tunes and adding harmonies to them. No one was interested in who exactly wrote which song or where a song came from. Even though some early country songs sound like Irish folk, their lyrics reflect an entirely different reality—that of the hardships of rural mountain life.

200 years before the first country record, country music defined the sound of everyday life in the mountains. Settlers adopted a big repertoire of songs, which they practiced in church, especially on

Sundays. Over time, harmonies evolved and the simple mountain tunes became sophisticated hymns. To that end, country music was strongly influenced by gospel.

But despite the popularity of country music among mountain settlers, the genre never left the villages until the early 20th century. This is where the Carter Family fits into the historical picture. A. P. Carter was born 1891 in Maces Springs, Virginia (now Hiltons, Virginia), in a poor family of seven brothers and sisters. He had a tremor in his hand since childhood. The other kids used to make fun of him for that, so his mother pulled him out of school.

A. P. started selling fruit trees. He spent his days walking across and between mountain villages, whistling tunes he had learned at church as a child. One day, he met a girl who sat on the porch of a shack, singing beautiful songs. This was Sara, who became A. P.'s wife in 1915. Later, A. P.'s brother married Sara's cousin, Maybelle, who played the guitar very well.

Around 1920, the three musicians formed a trio and started performing at local events and church gatherings. Sara played the autoharp, Maybelle was on the guitar, and A. P. sang backing vocals (occasionally, he sang the lead, and on many tracks, he didn't perform at all). Although all of them had been raised poor, they had solid musical skills. It was customary for every rural family in the 19th century to have at least a piano in their house. Notably, Maybelle invented what is known in the guitar world as the "Carter Scratch"—a guitar technique of playing the rhythm and the lead simultaneously.

Most songs the Carters sang sounded joyful and up-tempo, but a closer look at the lyrics reveals the sorrow of rural mountain life—

the poverty, the hardships, and the strong faith in God. It is not clear which songs were written by the Carters and which were traditional mountain tunes. At that time, however, no one paid too much attention to authorship.

Now that you know the historical roots of country music, you can understand the true meaning of the term "hillbilly". "Hillbilly music" went from being a derogatory term in the mid-1900s to being a musical brand around the end of the century.

Despite the obscure copyright around the Carters' music, it is known for sure that A. P. often went on song-seeking trips across the mountains. In 1935, the Carter Family published the songbook *Album of Smokey Mountain Ballads*, which contained the best of what A. P. found on his trips.

QUIZ

1. Where does country music come from originally?

   a. Nashville

   b. Texas

   c. The Appalachian Mountains

   d. Canada

2. In the pre-recording era, country music was sung by Black slaves.

   a. True

   b. False

3. In what venues did early country music develop?

   a. Factories

   b. Cotton fields

   c. Churches

   d. Urban houses

4. What was the main topic in early country music?

   a. Love affairs

   b. The hardships of rural life

   c. Political statements

   d. The hardships of slavery

5. Which genre was the biggest influence on early country music?

   a. African

   b. Classical

c. Vaudeville

d. Gospel

6. It was forbidden to sing during church maintenance in the 18th century.

   a. True

   b. False

7. It was also forbidden to sing during church gatherings.

   a. True

   b. False

8. Where did the Carter Family come from?

   a. Mountain villages

   b. Big cities

   c. Abroad

   d. Texas

9. What was peculiar about A. P. Carter?

   a. He was deaf

   b. He had a tremor in his hand

   c. He was blind

   d. He had a very harsh voice

10. How did A. P. Carter meet Sara?

   a. At a factory

   b. While selling fruit trees

   c. At a rehearsal

   d. Saw her at a wedding

11. Early country music consisted of only a few songs.

    a. True

    b. False

12. After getting together, the Carter Trio immediately went into the city to record.

    a. True

    b. False

13. How was Maybelle related to Sara?

    a. Sister

    b. Cousin

    c. Mother

    d. Daughter

14. The "Carter Scratch" was developed by whom?

    a. Maybelle

    b. Sara

    c. P.

    d. None of the above

15. All of the Carter Family's songs were original material.

    a. True

    b. False

16. The Carter Family's songs were joyful, both musically and lyrically.

    a. True

    b. False

17. "Hillbilly" has not always been a derisive term.

    a. True
    b. False

18. When was the Album of Smokey Mountain Ballads released?

    a. 1935
    b. 1927
    c. 1925
    d. 1945

19. Which Carter was known to regularly go on song-seeking trips?

    a. Maybelle
    b. P.
    c. Sara
    d. Josh

20. In the 19th century, most rural families had a piano in their house.

    a. True
    b. False

QUIZ ANSWER KEY

1. C- Appalachian Mountains

2. B- False

3. C- Churches

4. B- The hardships of rural life

5. D- Gospel

6. B- False

7. B- False

8. Mountain villages

9. He had a tremor in his hand

10. While selling fruit trees

11. B- False

12. B- False

13. B- Cousin

14. Maybelle

15. False

16. False

17. True

18. 1935

19. A. P.

20. True

CHAPTER 2

RISE OF THE HILLBILLY.

In 1926, the *Western Electric Company* invented the carbon microphone, which led to huge advances in the recording industry. Singers did not have to scream into tin cans anymore. The new microphones could also record more than one performer at a time. Moreover, it was now possible to make a complete record with a trunk's worth of equipment.

With these step-ups in recording technology, music producers became more confident and started looking for new opportunities around the US. Up until the mid-20s, record companies had focused primarily on classical and vaudeville music. Around 1927, however, producers began to notice a distinctive genre that the poor white people from the South played.

The South was perceived by urban citizens as the country (the countryside), and this is where the name of the genre came from. An idea sparked among entrepreneurs that this genre could be recorded and sold back to those same people who sang it at the rural churches.

Talent scout and record producer Ralph Peer was the first to capture this opportunity. He had been making recording trips in the South for some time, looking for authentic Black blues, so he was the right man to discover country music. In 1927, he went to Bristol, TN and offered $50 to any performer of 'mountain music' who would come and do a record.

A. P. Carter heard about the offer and immediately packed his bags. It took him a while to convince Sara and Maybelle, but eventually, they did arrive in Bristol on August 2, 1927. They had big trouble getting there—they blew a tire, had to walk and hide from the rain, etc. In any case, the date the Carters arrived in Bristol is known as the birthday of commercial country music. You may also hear musicians say that the Bristol Sessions were the 'Big Bang' of country.

Peer's temporary studio was in an old hat factory. When the Carters arrived, there was a queue of musicians waiting to be recorded. Many of them were good, but their repertoires consisted almost entirely of gospel hymns and blues. In a way, the Carters had no direct competition. Musicians were allowed one take only, or a maximum of two, if they were exceptionally good. The Carters, of course, were in the latter category.

The first song the Carters recorded was "Bury Me Under the Weeping Willow." There was no chance to hear what was being recorded in real-time. In other words, musicians had one take and also could not hear how it sounded. If anyone was to pass this test, they had to be really good. The Carters were so exceptional that they got two takes and got invited to a second session the next day. All in all, they recorded six songs at Peer's temporary studio.

After the sessions, Ralph Peer was not convinced that country music had any commercial value. He decided to stick to gospel and blues. He did, however, venture to try selling the Carter Family's music. They became a hit that no one had ever imagined. By 1948, they had recorded more than 200 songs and became the respected founders of country music.

To this day, Maybelle's guitar solo in "Wildwood Flower" is the textbook example of how country guitar sounds. Few guitarists in history have been as influential as Maybelle. She not only "created" the country style but also opened the doors for the development of early rock and roll.

Historians say that the early photographs of the Carter Family as a trio represent a whole era of American history and culture—the era of togetherness, simplicity, faith, hardships, and Victorian morals. The Carters looked like the epiphany of all that, but behind the scenes, their lives were torn apart by personal tensions. In 1933, Sara divorced A. P. and did not take the kids, which was very unusual at the time. A. P. never rebounded after that.

QUIZ

1. How many songs had the Carter Family recorded by 1948?

   c. 100

   d. 50

   e. 500

   f. 200

2. The technological advances in the early 20th century allowed for the development of portable recording studios.

   a. True

   b. False

3. Yet, the rapid technological changes discouraged music producers from investing in new artists.

   a. True

   b. False

4. Who was the original target audience for country music?

   a. White working class

   b. Black working class

   c. Rich white people

   d. Foreigners

5. The term "country" refers to what?

   a. USA

   b. Countryside

   c. The world as one

   d. None of the above

6. Southern audiences had no interest in country music, which reminded them of a poor past.

   a. True

   b. False

7. Maybelle and Sara Carter had to convince A. P. to record with Ralph Peer.

   a. True

   b. False

8. To what location was Ralph Peer's legendary recording trip in 1927?

   a. Bristol

   b. Dallas

   c. Nashville

   d. None of the above

9. When was the birthday of commercially-recorded country music?

   a. September 3, 1933

   b. August 2, 1927

   c. August 11, 1922

   d. July 13, 1939

10. Where was Ralph Peer's temporary studio located?

   a. Old hat factory

   b. Oil factory

   c. Forest

   d. Church

11. There was hardly any interest in Ralph Peer's recording sessions.

    a. True

    b. False

12. At Ralph Peer's recording session, musicians were allowed only one to two takes.

    a. True

    b. False

13. Which Carter Family song is the most influential among guitarists?

    a. "Cattle Call"

    b. "Wildwood Flower"

    c. "Bury Me Under the Weeping Willow"

    d. "On the Road Again"

14. Sara and A. P. Carter had a happy family life in the 30s.

    a. True

    b. False

15. How many songs did the Carters record in total at Peer's temporary sessions?

    a. 1

    b. 6

    c. 16

    d. 3

16. After the first day, Ralph Peer invited the Carter Family to a second session.

a. True

b. False

17. What was the first record by the Carter Family?

    a. "Singin' the Blues"

    b. "I Walk the Line"

    c. "Bury Me Under the Weeping Willow"

    d. "Pretty Polly"

18. How much per record did Ralph Peer pay at the legendary sessions?

    a. $500

    b. $50

    c. $5,000

    d. $5

19. In what year was the carbon microphone invented?

    a. 1926

    b. 1930

    c. 1935

    d. 1909

20. There was no way to hear what was being recorded in real-time at Peer's sessions.

    a. True

    b. False

QUIZ ANSWER KEY

1. D- 200

2. True

3. False

4. White working class

5. Countryside

6. False

7. False

8. Bristol

9. B - August 2, 1927

10. Old hat factory

11. False

12. False

13. "Wildwood Flower"

14. False

15. 6

16. True

17. Bury Me Under the Weeping Willow

18. $50

19. 1926

20. True

CHAPTER 3

MR. TWANG HIMSELF.

The Carters were the big hit of the Bristol Sessions, but there was one more musician there who would later write a whole chapter in the history of country music. His name was Jimmie Rodgers and he was from Mississippi. Believe it or not, Jimmie was the original singing kid with a guitar—a formula that has proved highly successful for the rest of modern music history.

From 1900 to 1930, life in the US changed rapidly. The Carters were not the only ones who came down from the mountains to look for opportunities. Thousands of people found work in the newly established factories and at railroad construction sites. Life conditions and morals were changing, and so was country music. The genre gradually began to lose its gospel element. Over time, there was less and less to say about the simple life in the mountains. The focus shifted from the isolated village person to the alienated working man in the city.

The USA was becoming an economic powerhouse, yet the South was slow to follow. Nothing much happened there, except for excruciating labor and poverty; only now it was in an urban setting. The "hillbilly" was now the poor guy at the bottom of the urban heap. Out of habit, the hillbilly sang old mountain songs, though they were becoming irrelevant.

Jimmie Rodgers was one of those poor working fellas. He worked at the Mississippi railroad line, which is where he listened to and played the blues. But he also added a very special ingredient to his singing—*yodeling*. Yodeling is typical of Austrian folk music, but no one before Rodgers had imagined it fitting into blues and country.

When he went to Peer's studio in 1927, Jimmie recorded two tracks that didn't sell very well. Sometime later, Jimmie decided to contact Peer and schedule another session. He was way more confident than before and had no shame emphasizing the distinctive feature of his singing—the *blue yodeling*, a term introduced by Jimmie and used to differentiate between Austrian and American yodeling.

The *Blue Yodel Sessions* went on from 1927 to 1933. Jimmie became hugely successful and influential, not only because of his yodeling but also because of his lyrics—which were very far from mountain hymns but very close to what was going on inside the hillbilly's head at the time. The most emblematic of those songs, "Blue Yodel (T for Texas)" sold more than half a million copies. Country music had started from the Carters' "weeping willow" and somehow arrived at the "pistols and trains" of Jimmie Rodgers.

Jimmie Rodgers is often said to have invented white blues. Indeed, he understood blues music very well. He and his father spent most of their lives banging the railroad tracks. Jimmie developed tuberculosis and had to quit the railroad work. That inspired him even further to pursue a full-time career in music. Soon after "Blue Yodel (T for Texas)," Jimmie became known as *The Singing Brakeman*—the first solo country star.

Apart from pistols and trains, Jimmie Rodgers shared many personal stories in his songs. This level of intimacy and honesty was not typical of country music at the time. But it appealed to listeners like nothing before had. This new sound and lyric constituted the *twang*—a vague term, still in use to today, to describe the vibe of country.

On the other hand, Jimmie unwillingly started a brand. Every new country singer began putting on a brakeman's uniform and singing bluesy tunes. Yet, few understood "the train songs" like Jimmie did.

In 1933, Jimmie Rodgers died of tuberculosis. Throughout his career, he toured the entire country and sold more than 20 million records. Unfortunately, his popularity had almost vanished by the end of his life and career.

QUIZ

1. Where was Jimmie Rodgers born?

   c. Texas

   d. Mississippi

   e. California

   f. New York

2. Jimmie Rodgers was the first solo singing country boy with a guitar.

   a. True

   b. False

3. Jimmie Rodgers represented what - through his music?

   a. The working-class man

   b. The emotional young boy

   c. The poor Black kid

   d. All the above

4. "Hillbilly" referred to religious leaders in the 30s.

   a. True

   b. False

5. Working-class white people listened to country in the 30s.

   a. True

   b. False

6. Country music did not lose its original gospel mountain vibe until the 60s.

a. True

b. False

7. The Carters were among the few who left the mountain village for the city.

a. True

b. False

8. Where did Jimmie Rodgers learn to sing the blues?

a. At the railroad line

b. At school

c. At home

d. At musical school

9. What was Jimmie Rodgers's first hit?

a. "Lady in Red"

b. "Train Song"

c. "Blue Yodel (T for Texas)"

d. "Give My Love to Rose"

10. Jimmie Rodgers's lyrics were strictly gospel.

a. True

b. False

11. Jimmie Rodgers introduced yodeling to country.

a. True

b. False

12. Original yodeling came from Austrian folk.

a. True

b. False

13. What caused Jimmie Rodgers to quit his railroad job?

    a. Opportunities

    b. Tuberculosis

    c. Scandals at work

    d. None of the above

14. What was the nickname Jimmie Rodgers got during his music career?

    a. The Train Roller

    b. The White Boy

    c. The Singing Brakeman

    d. The Cowboy

15. Jimmie Rodgers was discovered at the 1927 Bristol Sessions, where the Carters recorded.

    a. True

    b. False

16. "Blue yodeling" refers to European yodeling.

    a. True

    b. False

17. Jimmie Rodgers became a hit immediately after he was discovered.

    a. True

    b. False

18. Jimmie Rodgers's brakeman's uniform was ridiculed by other country musicians.

    a. True

    b. False

19. In what year did Jimmie Rodgers die?

   a. 1950

   b. 1933

   c. 1929

   d. 1941

20. "Twang" is a well-defined term in music theory.

   a. True

   b. False

QUIZ ANSWER KEY

1. B- Mississippi

2. True

3. The working-class man

4. False

5. True

6. False

7. False

8. At the railroad line

9. "Blue Yodel (T for Texas)"

10. False

11. True

12. True

13. Tuberculosis

14. The Singing Brakeman

15. True

16. False

17. False

18. False

19. 1933

20. False

CHAPTER 4

DID YOU KNOW?

THE SINGING COWBOY

Hollywood has never been too concerned with authenticity. In the late 20s, they laid their hands on country music and quickly managed to turn it into a factory-made product. First, they adopted the brakeman's uniform from Jimmie Rodgers. Second, they turned the idea of looking poor into a stage act. People like Rodgers composed their songs while listening to the rhythm of the train that leaves their home. In Hollywood's opinion, though, trains and iron ores were the symbols of American prosperity, and so it was no surprise to see singers dressed like brakemen singing about how rich the US was. But although the old pop—vaudeville—was dying and had to be replaced, this new trend didn't appeal to true country fans.

Before Hollywood country gained too much momentum, the Great Depression hit. There was huge turmoil in the US in 1929, and the last thing people wanted to see was an entertainer who praised the current economic model. The industry had to adjust quickly. Jimmy Rodgers, though, didn't stop recording and performing: he was the original brakeman, and his honesty and intimacy appealed to his audience, despite the national economic tragedy.

This is when Hollywood came up with the idea of *the cowboy*—a free man on a horse, with no job, and a pretty girl on his hands—the exact opposite of the typical struggling American in the 1930s. The singing cowboy hit Americans right through the heart, and in a way, defined commercial country music for the rest of history.

The most famous of these cowboys was Gene Autry. He was not only a great performer but also an extravagant dresser. Together with tailor and designer Nudie Cohn, Gene established the unprecedented brand of the flashy singing cowboy. Desperate and hopeful Americans accepted this brand wholeheartedly.

By the mid-30s, every country musician was dressed like a cowboy, no matter what they sang. The term "hillbilly" had already become derisive.

The root of the cowboy image, however, comes from Texas. Many Texas farms were destroyed in the 1930s, and thousands of Texans moved to LA. Interestingly though, the cowboy returned to Texas with renewed vigor once the economic recovery and the oil boom began. The first Texas cowboy superstar was Bob Wills—often called the king of Western swing—and his band *The Texas Playboys*.

At the same time, Nashville was trying to do things the old, hillbilly way. In 1925, the *Grand Ole Opry* was established. It was initially a live radio show, focused on authentic country music. Today, it is the most elite stage for any country performer. The *Opry*'s target audience in the 30s was those who needed a break from the fast-changing world and the superficiality of modernism.

The Nashville musician was a rural boy, who sang traditional country at the *Opry* and drank from a fruit jar. This naturally attracted rural audiences and older listeners. In reality, however, every performance at the *Opry* was carefully orchestrated, much like vaudeville shows.

Although Nashville singers did eventually start to wear cowboy hats, they were perceived as the antidote to LA cowboys. The topics in Nashville were not pretty girls and flashy cars. The *Opry* was about family, farm, church, etc. In this context, the first singing brothers emerged—boys dressed in shirts, who wanted to make their mothers proud.

It is worth mentioning George D. Hay, the founder and host of the *Opry*. He was an exceptionally smart man who stood behind the dress code and the scripts of the show. Hay found the best way to preserve traditional country and save it from being trodden down by modern trends.

QUIZ

1. Who was the early embodiment of Hollywood's idea of a cowboy?

    a. Johnny Cash

    b. P. Carter

    c. Jimmie Rodgers

    d. Gene Autry

2. In the eyes of Hollywood, trains and ores represented American prosperity.

    a. True

    b. False

3. After Jimmie Rodgers's death, looking poor turned into a commercial brand in country.

    a. True

    b. False

4. Who was Gene Autry's stylist?

    a. Nudie Cohn

    b. Christian Dior

    c. Jimmie Rodgers

    d. Marilyn Monroe

5. To be dressed as a cowboy in the 40s, you had to play traditional country.

    a. True

    b. False

6. Jimmie Rodgers's music became irrelevant once the Great Depression hit.

   a. True

   b. False

7. Hollywood's cowboy was an antidote to the everyday struggles of Americans.

   a. True

   b. False

8. Where does the original cowboy image come from?

   a. New Jersey

   b. Tennessee

   c. Texas

   d. California

9. How was Bob Wills' band called?

   a. The Honky Tonk Angels

   b. The Flying Burritos

   c. The Texas Playboys

   d. The Hollywood Underdogs

10. By the mid-30s, "hillbilly" had already become a derisive term.

   a. True

   b. False

11. Hollywood's cowboy fell from fame quickly after he was introduced.

   a. True

   b. False

12. Gene Autry was a humble dresser.

    a. True

    b. False

13. What was Nashville's most successful radio production in the 30s?

    a. Country Music Awards

    b. Grand Ole Opry

    c. Country Dance Week

    d. None of the above

14. Nashville's country radio shows were 100% impromptu.

    a. True

    b. False

15. The Nashville country singer of the 30s was almost the same as Hollywood's cowboy.

    a. True

    b. False

16. Bob Wills returned to Texas after gaining popularity in Hollywood.

    a. True

    b. False

17. Who was the host of the *Grand Ole Opry* in the 30s?

    a. Roy Acuff

    b. Johnny Cash

    c. George D. Hay

    d. None of the above

18. The first singing brother duos emerged in Nashville.

    a. True
    b. False

19. For how many years (approximately) did Nashville's successful country radio show air?

    a. 15
    b. 100
    c. 20
    d. 5

20. Vaudeville was at its peak in the early 40s.

    a. True
    b. False

QUIZ ANSWER KEY

1. D- Gene Autry

2. True

3. True

4. Nudie Cohn

5. False

6. False

7. True

8. Texas

9. The Texas Playboys

10. True

11. False

12. False

13. Grand Ole Opry

14. False

15. False

16. True

17. George D. Hay

18. False

19. 100

20. False

CHAPTER 5

THE RADIO, THE OPRY, AND THE HONKY TONK.

As you can see by now, the idea that country music came from Wild West cowboys, who wooed long-haired country girls, is rather mistaken. Similarly mistaken is the common perception of why the *Grand Ole Opry* became so popular. As the Great Depression hit in the early 30s, music sales plummeted. Working-class people had no money to purchase records, so they turned to radio. Radio offered free music and entertainment, and the *Opry* was the most appealing show. Listening to the *Opry* on Saturday night became a regular occasion for many small communities. More than a few country stars grew up in that atmosphere and got their first inspirations from the singers at the *Opry*.

The first household name at the *Opry* was Roy Acuff. Before joining the show, he struggled with his career because his singing was considered too old fashioned. He was perfect for George Hay's vision, though. Acuff sang traditional country songs, some of which were from the Carter Family's repertoire. In the eyes of the producers, Acuff was the perfect guy to promote traditional family values to a national audience.

On the other side of life, there were the factory and iron ore workers. Many of these workers weren't strictly family men, mainly because they worked far away from their families for long periods. Such people gradually got into the habit of visiting local bars after a hard-working day. These shady bars became known as "honky tonks." They rapidly grew in number after alcohol became legal again in 1933. Honky tonks had live country music.

But that country was way rougher than what could be heard at the *Opry* or even at Bob Wills' shows. The people who listened to it were rough too, so they refused to listen to anything with lyrics they considered too mellow. Fights took place when musicians were not honky tonk enough. Eventually, owners had to put nets around live bands to protect them.

Then, WWII began. The American workforce was allocated among weapon factories and the economic recovery started. But not the spiritual recovery. Honky tonks were now at the peak of their popularity, sheltering tired, drunk, and sad workers every night. Country bands had to start playing louder and harder. The need for amplifiers, mics, and electrified instruments arose. This is also when the strong drum beats and percussive guitar rhythms made their way into country music.

The war left a mark on traditional American morals, and the honky tonk was the place where these new morals were celebrated: drinking, cheating, fast driving, etc. The face of the new culture was Ernest Tubb—a country singer and womanizer, who owned a honky tonk.

Tubb's "Walking the Floor Over You" is considered the anthem of honky tonk music. The harsh way Tubb's guitar sounded was shocking to traditional country fans, but it was highly appropriate for honky tonk audiences.

Country music was now as far from the church as it could get. Honky tonk musicians sang about one-night stands, cheating wives, hangovers, gun fights, and others. The rules of love and relationships had changed a lot.

Younger audiences were also attracted to honky tonks. They were drawn by the sexual charge of this new style of country music. Floyd Tillman's "Slipping Around" (1949) is an ideal reflection of what had become of country in the 40s. It was not the first song about cheating, but it was the first one to praise rather than moralize it.

It didn't take long before honky tonk also became a battleground for the sexes. For the first time, women were not content with their drunken husbands and didn't hesitate to sing about it. The most notable example of this battle was Kitty Wells' "It Wasn't God Who Made Honky Tonk Angels" (1952).

QUIZ

1. What was the main reason behind the *Opry*'s success?

   a. Radio was free

   b. Country was a teenage vogue

   c. Naked females on stage

   d. None of the above

2. The *Opry* was a carefully orchestrated and well-produced show.

   a. True

   b. False

3. Who was the first famous singer of the *Opry*?

   a. Jimmie Rodgers

   b. Roy Acuff

   c. Hawkshaw Hawkins

   d. Johnny Cash

4. What bars gained popularity among the working class after the end of Prohibition?

   a. Vaudeville venues

   b. Honky Tonks

   c. Variety bars

   d. Jazz clubs

5. Working class bars in the 30s had live gospel-country music.

   a. True

   b. False

6. Factory workers in the 30s traveled with their families and listened to the *Opry* in their cars.

    a. True

    b. False

7. Female singers were not allowed in 40s country music.

    a. True

    b. False

8. The term "honky tonk" refers to a peculiar piano sound used in country music.

    a. True

    b. False

9. Which country song was the working-class bar anthem of the early 40s?

    a. "Blue Yodel (T for Texas)"

    b. "Walking the Floor Over You"

    c. "Jumpin' Jack Flash"

    d. "Live Forever"

10. Which of the following artists was a popular country singer and womanizer in the early 40s?

    a. Hank Williams

    b. Ernest Tubb

    c. Jimmie Rodgers

    d. P. Carter

11. The economic recovery after WWII diminished the popularity of working-class bars.

a. True

b. False

12. Country bands of the 40s adopted electric instruments and a harder sound.

a. True

b. False

13. Young people were attracted to working-class country bars in the 40s by what?

a. Sexual opportunities

b. Bar design

c. Secret political meetings

d. None of the above

14. 40s country music served as a battleground for the sexes.

a. True

b. False

15. In what year was Floyd Tillman's "Slipping Around" released?

a. 1941

b. 1949

c. 1933

d. 1946

16. Before the *Opry*, Roy Acuff had already become a superstar.

a. True

b. False

17. Ernest Tubb's guitar sound was a reminder of Maybelle Carter's music.

a. True

b. False

18. Country music of the 40s protested the demoralization of American society.

   a. True

   b. False

19. At 40s working-class beer joints, musicians were protected from fights by on-stage nets.

   a. True

   b. False

20. Many country music stars of the 20th century grew up listening to the *Opry* on Saturdays.

   a. True

   b. False

QUIZ ANSWER KEY

1. Radio was free

2. True

3. Roy Acuff

4. Honky Tonks

5. False

6. False

7. False

8. False

9. B- "Walking the Floor Over You"

10. B- Ernest Tubb

11. B- False

12. True

13. Sexual opportunities

14. True

15. 1949

16. False

17. False

18. False

19. True

20. True

CHAPTER 6

BROTHER ACTS AND BLUEGRASS.

Let's step back from honky tonk and revisit the *Opry*, and specifically those brothers who made their mothers proud. As mentioned before, the invention of new microphones allowed singers to sing more quietly and develop much more intricate lines. This is exactly what the Stanley Brothers and the Louvin Brothers did: they introduced complex vocal harmony to country music.

Carter Stanley died in 1966 and left Ralph Stanley to a solo career. You have probably heard of Ralph's song "Man of Constant Sorrow"—yes, he did the original version in the 50s. It is unknown, however, who wrote this song and how old it is.

The Louvin Brothers, with their perfectly pitched voices, took vocal harmony to even higher heights. Much like the Stanley Brothers, they focused on old songs and attempted to re-arrange them into new and sophisticated pieces. Their most famous song was "The Knoxville Girl" (1956)—an Americanized version of the 19th century Irish murder ballad, "The Wexford Girl."

To realize how intertwined with Victorian morals traditional country music was, notice that in the story of the Wexford Girl, the murderer escapes, while in the American version, justice prevails. It is unclear why "The Knoxville Girl" became such a big hit. The fact is that it gave birth to an entire subgenre of country music, still performed today—murder country ballads.

Eventually, the Louvin Brothers split up over drinking problems. Sadly, the history of country music shows that brothers tend to break up. Today, there are almost no brother duos in country, nor is there any demand for such duos.

Another notable brother act from that era was the Monroe Brothers. They split up in 1938 and went their separate musical ways. Bill Monroe had no intention of quitting music and quickly formed a band, which he called The Blue Grass Boys—after the Bluegrass region in Kentucky, Bill's homeland. This is how *bluegrass* was born.

Bluegrass was still country but way more energetic and aggressive. The rules were to sound authentic, like the lone fellow singing on a mountain hill, to use no electric instruments and drums, and to be energetic. To that end, there were no love songs in bluegrass, especially considering how Bill Monroe "slammed" his mandolin.

In 1945, banjo player Earl Scruggs joined Bill Monroe's band. This is when bluegrass was defined as a separate genre. Earl played the banjo, which had been perceived as a comedian's instrument, so differently and so masterfully that no one even speaks of banjo music before Earl Scruggs anymore. Technically speaking, Earl added the third finger of the right hand and the speed to the instrument.

After two and a half years, Earl Scruggs left Bill Monroe, together with guitarist Lester Flat. They weren't the first. Bill treated his musicians so badly that he needed a new member every two weeks, on average. For example, he forced his musicians to do farm work in their free time, so that they could stay close to the authentic country life.

Bill Monroe was known to criticize every musician who dared to call themselves a bluegrass performer. Monroe thought that no one could understand real bluegrass and that the genre would be gone after his death. History, however, proved him quite wrong.

QUIZ

1. Which of the following is an early example of a brother act in country music?

   a. Blues Brothers

   b. Allman Brothers

   c. Louvin Brothers

   d. Simon and Garfunkel

2. Brother acts were first introduced at the *Opry*.

   a. True

   b. False

3. Country brothers promoted traditional values and morals.

   a. True

   b. False

4. What was the main reason behind the sophistication in vocal harmony in the 40s and 50s?

   a. The rising popularity of jazz

   b. Technological developments in recording gear

   c. Improved education

   d. None of the above

5. Who released "Man of Constant Sorrow" for the first time?

   a. Ralph Stanley

   b. Hank Williams

   c. Johnny Cash

   d. Soggy Bottom Boys

6. Carter Stanley was the original composer behind "Man of Constant Sorrow."

   a. True

   b. False

7. The Louvin Brothers were innovators in vocal harmony.

   a. True

   b. False

8. The first murder ballads in country became popular in the 40s.

   a. True

   b. False

9. Which of the following songs was originally released by the Louvin Brothers?

   a. "Bury Me Under the Weeping Willow"

   b. "Man of Constant Sorrow"

   c. "Jolene"

   d. "The Knoxville Girl"

10. The Louvin Brothers performed until 2010.

   a. True

   b. False

11. Brother acts are a successful formula, still used in country music today.

   a. True

   b. False

12. Bill Monroe created bluegrass.

   a. True

   b. False

13. The genre bluegrass is named after what?

    a. A musical instrument

    b. A region in Kentucky

    c. A drug

    d. A religious figure

14. What did Bill Monroe make his musicians do after work?

    a. Kidnap domestic animals

    b. Take drugs

    c. Do farm work

    d. None of the above

15. What instrument did Bill Monroe play?

    a. Mandolin

    b. Piano

    c. Drums

    d. Upright bass

16. Bluegrass relied on electric instruments and slow arrangements.

    a. True

    b. False

17. Who was the legendary banjo player that defined bluegrass sound?

    a. Hawkshaw Hawkins

    b. Steve Earle

    c. Earl Scruggs

    d. Bill Monroe

18. That same banjo player formed a duo with which guitarist in the 40s?

a. Lester Flat

b. Bill Monroe

c. Johnny Cash

d. Randy Travis

19. When did the Monroe Brothers split up?

a. 1938

b. 1949

c. 1966

d. 1931

20. In the song "The Wexford Girl," justice prevails over the murderer.

a. True

b. False

QUIZ ANSWER KEY

1. Louvin Brothers

2. True

3. True

4. Technological developments in recording gear

5. Ralph Stanley

6. False

7. True

8. True

9. "The Knoxville Girl"

10. False

11. False

12. True

13. A region in Kentucky

14. Do farm work

15. Mandolin

16. False

17. Earl Scruggs

18. Lester Flat

19. 1938

20. False

CHAPTER 7

HANK WILLIAMS.

The US was victorious after the war was over. As discussed before, these were odd times of economic prosperity against the background of broken homes and morals. But in this twisted honky tonk era, country music found its biggest star ever—Hank Williams. Born in poor rural Alabama in 1923, Hank discovered music through his mother, who was a church organist. This is where his gospel influence came from. His other influence was the blues, the other spirit of the South.

Hank was 8 when his father left home. Then, he and his mother moved to Georgiana. Hank started working at the railway station, selling peanuts and shining shoes. This is where he met his childhood musical hero, Rufus Payne. Payne was a 'blues' musician and a popular alcoholic in town.

Rufus Payne taught Hank the blues guitar. Hank once claimed that his hit "Move it on Over" (1947) was based on a guitar riff that Payne showed him as a child. This song is also thought by many historians to be the first rock and roll song. It is suspiciously similar to "Rock Around the Clock," which came out ten years later.

Another huge influence on Hank Williams was Roy Acuff from the *Grand Ole Opry*. Hank was impressed by how honest and emotional

Acuff's singing was. This sparked Hank's dream to play at the *Opry* one day.

Hank Williams created modern country music. This is great for us, but it was a disaster for Nashville at the time because Hank was no pretender. His songs were heartbreaking and true, and strongly reminded of the lost hillbilly soul of country music—exactly what the music industry establishment was running away from, under the pressure of modern trends.

Hank Williams did get to the *Grand Ole Opry* but was soon fired for being unreliable and drunk. His destructive alcoholism ruined both his career and put an end to his life. Some say that Rufus Payne introduced Hank not only to blues, but also to alcohol.

As an adult musician, Hank started in Nashville, with the help of producer Fred Rose. He quickly became a star and sold millions of records. Fans called him the "embodiment of honky tonk." In his early records, it is easy to spot how inspired Hank was by Ernest Tubb's work during the war years. Yet, the deep sorrow in Hank's songs cannot be compared to anything before or after.

In his personal life, Hank Williams struggled with marital problems and chronic back pain. Part of the reason why he drank was to relieve this pain. He was an exceptionally sensitive and loving person. Eventually, he divorced his wife Audrey, whom he loved very much. His greatest songs were inspired by this conflict. Although he did find new love over time, he never managed to forget Audrey, and this shone through the lyrics of many of his ballads.

Hank Williams's big breakthrough was in 1949, with his song "Lovesick Blues". The song was out of meter, and the producers were strongly against that. It did, however, become one of the greatest country hits ever. Hank was known as an unreliable drunk within the industry, but that song changed everyone's minds. Even the *Opry* hired him as a regular.

Eventually, Hank burned all his bridges, and even honky tonks were hesitant to hire him, all because of his alcoholism. In 1953, he died of a heart attack, after mixing alcohol with morphine and sedatives. He died on New Year's Eve, at the back of a car, on his way to a gig in Ohio. His last legacy was "Your Cheating Heart" (1952), dedicated to Audrey.

QUIZ

1. What instrument did Hank Williams's mother play?

    a. Church organ

    b. Banjo

    c. Mandolin

    d. Drums

2. Hank Williams learned gospel through his mother.

    a. True

    b. False

3. How old was Hank Williams when he moved to Georgiana?

    a. 12

    b. 8

    c. 24

    d. 3

4. What was Hank Williams's job as a child?

    a. Cleaner at a guitar factory

    b. Peanut seller

    c. Church cleaner

    d. Car washer

5. Who was Hank Williams's biggest blues influence as a child?

    a. Lead Belly

    b. Robert Johnson

    c. John Lee Hooker

    d. Rufus Payne

6. As a child, Hank Williams was inspired to get to the *Opry* and be like Roy Acuff.

    a. True

    b. False

7. Hank Williams is often referred to as the creator of modern country music.

    a. True

    b. False

8. The music industry establishment wholeheartedly welcomed Hank Williams's pure country style.

    a. True

    b. False

9. Which Hank Williams song was inspired by his childhood blues hero?

    a. "Move it on Over"

    b. "Your Cheating Heart"

    c. "I'm So Lonesome I Could Cry"

    d. "Country Roads"

10. As an adult, Hank Williams was notably fired from what show for being an alcoholic?

    a. Grand Ole Opry

    b. The Porter Wagoner Show

    c. The Ed Sullivan Show

    d. None of the above

11. Nevertheless, Hank Williams's alcoholism never caused him too much trouble.

a. True

b. False

12. Hank Williams's early recordings remind of honky tonker Ernest Tubb.

    a. True

    b. False

13. Who was the first Nashville producer to help Hank Williams?

    a. Chet Atkins

    b. Fred Rose

    c. Owen Bradley

    d. Tompall Glaser

14. The song "Rock Around the Clock" is suspiciously similar to which Hank Williams's song?

    a. "Lovesick Blues"

    b. "Your Cheating Heart"

    c. "Move it on Over"

    d. "Ride on"

15. In what year was Hank Williams's "Lovesick Blues" released?

    a. 1961

    b. 1949

    c. 1954

    d. 1951

16. Hank Williams was able to quickly forget his wife Audrey after their divorce.

    a. True

    b. False

17. Hank Williams struggled with marital problems and what else?

    a. Cancer

    b. Knee pain

    c. Chronic back pain

    d. None of the above

18. "Lovesick Blues" was out of meter and producers were hesitant to release it.

    a. True

    b. False

19. In what year did Hank Williams die?

    a. 1953

    b. 1960

    c. 1970

    d. 1949

20. Hank Williams learned about alcohol from Rufus Payne.

    a. True

    b. False

QUIZ ANSWER KEY

1. Church organ

2. True

3. 8

4. Peanut seller

5. Rufus Payne

6. True

7. True

8. False

9. "Move it on Over"

10. Grand Ole Opry

11. False

12. True

13. Fred Rose

14. "Move it on Over"

15. 1949

16. False

17. Chronic back pain

18. True

19. 1953

20. True

CHAPTER 8

THE END OF HONKY TONK.

After his death, Hank Williams became even more famous than when he was alive. There were more than 20,000 people at his funeral. The country music industry had a new hero but also now had to live up to his authenticity. Someone had to continue what Hank had started. Enter Ray Price, Hank's housemate. On the night Hank died, Ray was playing in a club 50 miles away from the death scene.

Ray Price was determined to keep honky tonk alive. He and Hank had been good friends and had written some songs together. Ray joined Hank's band and started touring. He was hugely successful, and country fans adored his resemblance to Hank Williams.

But before too long, Ray Price got tired of being compared to Hank Williams. Without too much fuss, he left Hank's band and went on to seek a new sound. Around the mid-50s, he joined the Cherokee Cowboys, where he was free to develop his own, unique style.

The Cherokee Cowboys were an unprecedented success. In 1956, they had their first hit "Crazy Arms," which sold more than a million copies and remained No. 1 on the country charts for 20 weeks.

The Cherokee Cowboys also laid the foundation of new country and rock and roll drumming. In their songs "City Lights" (1958) and

"Heartaches by the Number" (1959), they introduced the 4/4 shuffle beat to commercial music for the first time in history.

Ray's style became the premier brand of honky tonk, but there was yet another country star out there that had been Hank Williams's direct competition. His name was Lefty Frizzell. Born in the poor part of Texas, Lefty sang honest songs about his tough childhood. But there was also a feeling of danger around Lefty Frizzell. Naturally, he attracted thousands of young women to his audience.

In 1947, Lefty was sent to prison for having sex with an underage girl. At that time, he was already married. He didn't want to lose his wife and he wrote poems to her from the prison cell. One of these poems—"I Love You a Thousand Ways"—became a massive country hit when it was recorded in 1959.

Lefty's career lasted for 25 years. All in all, he registered 13 Top 10 hits. His bluesy and powerful singing technique became an inspiration for generations of musicians in all genres. But he was never able to sustain the success from the early 50s. In 1951, he and Hank Williams toured together, but no one lived to tell the stories from that tour.

On the other side of these honky tonkers was Hollywood. Hollywood took a lot from honky tonk, and vice versa. The industry's flashy cowboy was alive and well, and he was now even more of a brand than he was in the 30s and 40s. The singing cowboy had become *the rhinestone cowboy*—rich, muscular, and slightly arrogant. The rhinestone cowboy sang 'dance country' and had female dancers on stage behind him. But the rhinestone costume was also the dress code of honky tonk. Stylist Nudie Cohn (who we learned of in a previous chapter) was the creator of the rhinestone cowboy costume.

Meanwhile, there was a kid from Mississippi who was inspired by both the honky tonkers and the cowboys. He had a dream to be the next Hank Williams. And he did make to the *Opry*. They called him the "Hillbilly Cat." His country music dreams were coming true. To prove himself worthy of the title "country singer," he released a cover of Bill Monroe's "Blue Moon of Kentucky" in 1954. That kid's name was Elvis Presley.

QUIZ

1. Which one was a notable honky tonk musician and roommate of Hank Williams?

    a. Chuck Berry

    b. Johnny Cash

    c. Ray Price

    d. Waylon Jennings

2. Hank Williams was more famous posthumously than when he was alive.

    a. True

    b. False

3. There were more than 10,000 people at Hank Williams's funeral.

    a. True

    b. False

4. Which of the following musicians continued touring with Hank Williams's band after the funeral?

    a. Hawkshaw Hawkins

    b. Ray Price

    c. Lefty Frizzell

    d. None

5. Which of these was the Cherokee Cowboys' first hit?

    a. "Your Cheating Heart"

    b. "Crazy Arms"

c. "Achy Breaky Heart"

d. "Lovesick Blues"

6. The Cherokee Cowboys wanted to detach from Hank Williams's sound.

   a. True

   b. False

7. The Cherokee Cowboys introduced the 4/4 shuffle beat into country music.

   a. True

   b. False

8. Which of the following musicians was considered Hank Williams's direct competition?

   a. Lefty Frizzell

   b. Ray Price

   c. Ernest Tubb

   d. None of the above

9. Which of the following songs was written by Hank Williams's direct competition?

   a. "Lovesick Blues"

   b. "I Love You a Thousand Ways"

   c. "Hey, Good Looking"

   d. "Cotton Fields of Home"

10. Who wrote "Heartaches by the Number" (1959)?

    a. The Cherokee Cowboys

    b. Hank Williams

    c. Kitty Wells

    d. Earl Scruggs

11. In his career, honky tonker Lefty Frizzell hit the Top 10 charts 13 times.

    a. True

    b. False

12. Lefty Frizzell produced Ray Price's music.

    a. True

    b. False

13. For what crime did Lefty Frizzell go to prison?

    a. Copyright infringement

    b. Sex with an underage girl

    c. Murder

    d. Document fraud

14. Lefty Frizzell wrote his biggest hit while he was in prison in 1959.

    a. True

    b. False

15. Who stood behind the rhinestone cowboy apparel?

    a. Lefty Frizzell

    b. Hank Williams

    c. Nudie Cohn

    d. Andy Warhol

16. "Rhinestone cowboy" referred to 50s honky tonkers from the South.

    a. True

    b. False

17. Elvis Presley dreamed of being the next Hank Williams.

   a. True

   b. False

18. Elvis Presley was on *Opry's* stage for a while. They called him the "Hillbilly Cat."

   a. True

   b. False

19. Who wrote the original of Presley's "Blue Moon of Kentucky"?

   a. Ray Price

   b. Lefty Frizzell

   c. Bill Monroe

   d. Hank Williams

20. Lefty Frizzell attracted women with his dangerous look.

   a. True

   b. False

QUIZ ANSWER KEY

1. Ray Price

2. True

3. True

4. Ray Price

5. "Crazy Arms"

6. True

7. True

8. Lefty Frizzell

9. "I Love You a Thousand Ways"

10. The Cherokee Cowboys

11. True

12. False

13. Sex with an underage girl

14. True

15. Nudie Cohn

16. False

17. True

18. True

19. Bill Monroe

20. True

CHAPTER 9

TIME TO REDEFINE.

The 1950s saw serious social and moral changes in everyday American life. Country music tracked and followed these changes. There were the honky tonkers and there were the rhinestone cowboys. But there was also Nashville. What used to be the breeding ground for old authentic country had now become the powerhouse of commercial 'suburban music'. *The Opry* had lost its reputation with true country fans, and country music was breaking apart.

In addition, country had lost much of its hillbilly vibe by allowing electric instruments and drumbeats. And then along came rock and roll, led by no other than former country boy Elvis Presley. Legends like Flat & Scruggs and the Stanley Brothers went from $1,000 to $100 a night.

Suddenly, both the honky tonkers and the cowboys looked irrelevant. Teenagers were after rock and roll, and the industry had to follow the trend. Country music was for old suburban people. And even that suburban country was made in Nashville and was far from authentic. To define "the real old country music," people started using the term bluegrass—which, as you already know, has a different original meaning.

Nashville now had a mocking attitude towards bluegrass. That music was about farms and churches, and the new audiences weren't concerned with such topics. It was either Elvis or the New Nashville Sound. Even "twangy" became a derisive term.

In a way, country musicians had no choice but to jump on Nashville's train. Nashville's idea was to remove the twang, add modern arrangements, and put an alternative to rock and roll out on the market. That new sound had to be radio-friendly, smooth, metered, more sophisticated, and with no fiddles, banjos, or anything like that.

The architects of the New Nashville Sound were Owen Bradley and Chet Atkins. In 1957, a former honky tonker from Texas—Jim Reeves—contacted them to ask for work. They quickly ran him through the re-clothing room and put him in the studio. Then, the ultimate hit song "Four Walls" was recorded.

In the studio, Jim Reeves developed a strange habit of putting his lips on the microphone and singing quietly, as if talking. He had a mesmerizing baritone voice. The producers loved that. Whether they knew it or not at the time, this way of singing would become the foundation of mainstream pop for years to come.

The members of Atkins's and Bradley's session band were known as "the A-Team." The vision of the architects was to build a production line for music. The singer would come, the stylists would fix him, the composers and producers would put together some songs, and the A-Team would record with the singer. No beer joints, no farms, no yodeling, or any of this stuff. This production line formula is still used today in mainstream pop.

By 1960, the formula was refined, and the architects applied it to child singing prodigy Brenda Lee. Her single "I'm Sorry" (1960) has sold more than 15 million records, as of 2020. The new sound was a reflection of suburban family aspirations. The new country appealed to people who did not necessarily go out drinking every night.

And this didn't even start in the 50s. Farm boys had become international superstar's years before Jim Reeves. Honky tonker Eddy Arnold joined the country club with "The Cattle Call" in 1944. He grew up even poorer than Hank Williams but always wanted to reach fame; he never really thought of himself as a honky tonk loser. It was nice to receive support from true country fans, but you had to record country pop to make ends meet. And more often than not, there was a trade-off.

QUIZ

1. In the 50s, Nashville focused primarily on what audiences?

    a. Rural
    b. Suburban
    c. Honky Tonk
    d. Foreign

2. In the 50s, country music returned to gospel.

    a. True
    b. False

3. Rock and roll never became as popular as country because Elvis Presley was a country boy.

    a. True
    b. False

4. In the mid-50s, Flat & Scruggs lost popularity because they lost technical playing ability.

    a. True
    b. False

5. Which of the following country acts was still performing in the mid-50s?

    a. P. Carter's Quintet
    b. Hank Williams
    c. Jimmie Rodgers
    d. Stanley Brothers

6. The Nashville establishment fought to rescue traditional country, despite the new trends; and they succeeded.

    a. True

    b. False

7. *The Grand Ole Opry* never gave up on its original hillbilly-gospel orientation.

    a. True

    b. False

8. Once early rock and roll hit the charts, bluegrass became a definition of what?

    a. Old country music

    b. Bill Monroe's music

    c. New country styles

    d. The Nashville Sound

9. Which one of the following producers is considered an architect of the New Nashville Sound?

    a. George Martin

    b. Fred Rose

    c. Lefty Frizzell

    d. Chet Atkins

10. Urban teenage audiences of the mid-50s were mostly interested in what?

    a. Rock and roll

    b. Authentic country

    c. Bluegrass

    d. Murder ballads

11. The New Nashville Sound was twangy.

    a. True

    b. False

12. The New Nashville Sound was designed as an alternative to rock and roll.

    a. True

    b. False

13. Who was the famous artist who sang "Four Walls" (1957)?

    a. George Jones

    b. Jim Reeves

    c. Hank Williams

    d. Ray Price

14. "Four Walls" introduced what interesting technique to pop singing?

    a. Loud screaming

    b. Quiet singing, far from the microphone

    c. Quiet singing, close to the microphone

    d. Scat singing

15. Which of the following Nashville singers was a famous baritone?

    a. Ray Price

    b. Elvis Presley

    c. Jim Reeves

    d. Frank Costello

16. The A-Team session band was not a part of Nashville's music production line.

a. True

b. False

17. Who sang "The Cattle Call" in 1944?

a. Waylon Jennings

b. Ray Price

c. Eddy Arnold

d. Hank Williams

18. How many copies of "I'm Sorry" has Brenda Lee sold so far?

a. 2 million

b. 15 million

c. 1 million

d. 200,000

19. When was Brenda Lee's "I'm Sorry" released?

a. 1952

b. 1938

c. 1970

d. 1960

20. Early rock and roll made rhinestone cowboys and honky tonkers look even fancier.

a. True

b. False

QUIZ ANSWER KEY

1. Suburban

2. False

3. False

4. False

5. Stanley Brothers

6. False

7. False

8. Old country music

9. Chet Atkins

10. Rock and roll

11. False

12. True

13. Jim Reeves

14. Quiet singing, close to the microphone

15. Jim Reeves

16. False

17. Eddy Arnold

18. 15 million

19. 1960

20. False

CHAPTER 10

IN THE SUBURBS.

In 1964, Jim Reeves died in a plane crash. By that time, true country fans had given up on Nashville and the New Sound concept. Music that was intentionally designed not to offend anyone could not be called country—it was not only far from the mountain songs. It was far from anything country had ever been.

For better or worse, the king of honky tonk—Ray Price—also moved to a Nashville studio. In 1967, he recorded "Danny Boy", and honky tonk fans were shocked. Later, at a concert in San Antonio, TX, fans spat on him and trashed the venue. Thirty-two were arrested. Such turmoil was comparable only to Bob Dylan's going electric.

But on the other hand, what would have happened to country if it wasn't for the New Nashville Sound? Would it have survived the rock and roll earthquake? Probably not. Nashville built its model around teasing the depression of suburban American adults and country completely lost touch with its roots. But at least it was out there, in some form—unlike vaudeville.

More importantly, the new country carefully tracked social and moral norms. Singers were getting more and more emotional and dramatic—like never before. Some claim that no one would have heard of Willie Nelson's "Crazy" if it wasn't for Patsy Cline's cover in 1961. Country music was lonesome, reflecting both the disasters and the glamor of metropolitan life.

Women had finally found a platform their voices, although tables had turned quite a bit since honky tonk girl Kitty Wells. Divorce rates were at an all-time high. Single moms were struggling in a world dominated by men. But at least they were allowed to sing about their troubles. And the pill had also come along.

Loretta Lynn and Tammy Wynette were two emblematic female voices of the 60s. They sang about the hardships of raising kids, divorce, remarriage, etc. It was not accepted in country music to sing about such things, especially according to Nashville producers. But listeners loved it, so the industry suddenly adopted and sheltered this new type of rebellious female country. It was now a part of the suburban repertoire.

Loretta Lynn was the daughter of a coalminer. She grew up poor and moved to the city to look for opportunity. She ran away from rural poverty only to find a different kind of disaster—the whirlpool of urban life. She got married at 13 and had four children by 18. Life was hard for her, and there was no doubt she was completely honest in her songs—check out "You Ain't Woman Enough (To Take My Man)" (1966).

Similarly, Tammy Wynette came from the cotton fields of the South. She also wrote sad female songs, until she married former honky tonk singer George Jones in 1969. The married couple was perfect for Nashville's vision of country pop. As a duo, they sang about suburban family life, just like in the old days of Jim Reeves.

But by the end of the 60s, the whole idea of family was under fire. Tammy and George did have a large audience, but the people in that audience could not relate to the mellow marital songs that the couple wrote and performed. In 1975, Tammy and George divorced, and George went back to his former honky tonk lifestyle. His song "He Stopped Loving Her Today" (1980) is dedicated to the divorce.

All in all, new pop country fans were not concerned with crop failures, horses, and cowboy hats. The architects at Nashville were very aware of that, and they continued to shape their production-line music accordingly. Nashville also had political support. Nixon's 1974 speech at the *Opry* was not the first republican speech there.

QUIZ

1. Renowned Nashville singer Jim Reeves died in what year?

    a. 1971

    b. 1962

    c. 1964

    d. 1959

2. By the time Jim Reeves died, country fans had adopted the New Nashville Sound.

    a. True

    b. False

3. In the 60s, honky tonker Ray Price switched to what genre?

    a. Rock and roll

    b. New Nashville Sound

    c. Gospel

    d. None the above

4. What hit song did Ray Price record in 1967?

    a. "Lovesick Blues"

    b. "Danny Boy"

    c. "Heartaches by the Number"

    d. "City Lights"

5. Where did Ray Price's notorious 1967 live gig take place?

    a. New York

    b. Georgiana

c. Nashville

d. San Antonio

6. The New Nashville Sound was based around the depression of suburban American adults.

    a. True

    b. False

7. New Nashville Sound artists were less emotional and thus more approachable by the youth.

    a. True

    b. False

8. Who was the original author of the country hit "Crazy"?

    a. Willie Nelson

    b. Patsy Cline

    c. Loretta Lynn

    d. Chet Atkins

9. Which of the following was a famous female honky tonk artist?

    a. Sara Carter

    b. Aretha Franklin

    c. Vera Lynn

    d. Kitty Wells

10. What was one topic that Tammy Wynette sang about that was unusual for the time?

    a. Divorce

    b. Job seeking

    c. Sexuality

    d. None of the above

11. Country music of the 60s disempowered female singers.

    a. True

    b. False

12. Loretta Lynn's lyrics were traditional rhymes from old gospel songs.

    a. True

    b. False

13. The 60s Nashville establishment eventually adopted female country.

    a. True

    b. False

14. Which of the following songs is by Loretta Lynn?

    a. "It Wasn't God Who Made Honky Tonk Angels"

    b. "Live Forever"

    c. "You Ain't Woman Enough (To Take My Man)"

    d. "Sitting Here"

15. When did Tammy Wynette marry George Jones?

    a. 1959

    b. 1961

    c. 1969

    d. 1973

16. Loretta Lynn's childhood was happier compared to other women in country at that time.

    a. True

    b. False

17. Which song did George Jones dedicate to his divorce with Tammy Wynette?

　　a. "Honky Tonk Heroes"

　　b. "Kiss an Angel Good Morning"

　　c. "He Stopped Loving Her Today"

　　d. "Rocking Years"

18. Tammy Wynette and George Jones were outspoken rebels against the New Nashville Sound.

　　a. True

　　b. False

19. When was Nixon's famous speech at the *Grand Ole Opry*?

　　a. 1974

　　b. 1977

　　c. 1976

　　d. 1970

20. The New Nashville Sound helped country music survive the rock and roll earthquake.

　　a. True

　　b. False

QUIZ ANSWER KEY

1. 1964

2. False

3. New Nashville Sound

4. "Danny Boy"

5. San Antonio

6. True

7. False

8. Willie Nelson

9. Kitty Wells

10. Divorce

11. False

12. False

13. True

14. "You Ain't Woman Enough (To Take My Man)"

15. 1969

16. False

17. "He Stopped Loving Her Today"

18. False

19. 1974

20. True

CHAPTER 11

BLUEGRASS NEVER DIED.

Bill Monroe created bluegrass, and years later, Nashville completely anathematized it. As you already know, the term bluegrass was then used to refer to outdated country music. But the 60s had a different opinion on that topic. The US had a new political direction, and social tastes were changing rapidly. Suddenly, young people were more interested in authenticity than in entertainment. And what could be more authentic than bluegrass?

Before too long, bluegrass became the favorite genre of anti-consumerism and anti-industrialization movements. Bluegrass was authentic and very close to the roots of real country music, which used to be about the hardships of the working man. Somehow, the lack of popularity and glamor in bluegrass made it one of the most popular genres in the 60s. All this was a matter of attitude, though. Bluegrass country never actually had political lyrics.

The 60s pulled some big country names out of the drawer. Ralph Stanley's "Man of Constant Sorrow" was the anthem of the revival. Flat & Scruggs went back to touring. Even the Carters returned to the spotlight. Maybelle performed with her daughters, and Sara would also join them occasionally. Unfortunately, A. P. did not live long enough to witness all this. He died in 1960.

Soon enough, a new generation of bluegrass artists was on its way. One notable example was Ricky Skaggs, a singer and multi-instrumentalist. Ricky was a great innovator, but he was also no stranger to the masters of bluegrass. Born in 1954, he had already played on stage with Bill Monroe before turning 10. By the 70s, he became an opening act for Ralph Stanley's Clinch Mountain Boys.

In the 70s, Ricky Skaggs joined the high-profile country singer Emmylou Harris. Their collaboration unlocked an ocean of bluegrass to the world's music audiences. Emmylou had the voice, the phrase, and the presence, and Ricky was a bluegrass encyclopedia. Who would have thought of covering the Louvin Brothers in the 70s? And who would have thought these covers would turn into international hits?

Emmylou Harris and Ricky Skaggs pulled rock fans to country and took these fans way back to the Carter Family. Rock and bluegrass became friends. This new environment opened the doors for mega artists like Alison Krauss. Yes, the new bluegrass was light years away from Bill Monroe, but it was made up of the same elements and flavors: acoustic instruments, no drums, pure country lyrics, etc.

Alison Krauss made bluegrass more popular than it had ever been. She signed with the small independent label Rounder Records at 14 and has remained with them ever since. In the goal-oriented, cash-hungry world of the 80s, Alison was a twinkling star, who fought to preserve the traditions of true country music.

Alison Krauss is also famous for participating in the soundtracks of *O Brother, Where Art Thou?* (2000) and *Cold Mountain* (2003). She is often praised for being the savior of bluegrass and country music.

Another famous artist who dug deep into bluegrass was Gillian Welch. She denied participating in the highly commercialized Nashville game of the 90s and started her independent career with musical partner David Rawlings. Gillian swam to the emotional and spiritual depths of country, from the time before it became an industry. Her freedom resulted from her founding of her own record label; she didn't have to obey Nashville rules.

Gillian Welch's song "Caleb Meyer" (1998) is often called "the revenge of the Knoxville girl." For the first time in country music history, there was a female country ballad.

QUIZ

1. The Nashville establishment of the 60s adopted and produced a lot of bluegrass.

    a. True
    b. False

2. 60s youth were interested in bluegrass and old bluegrass artists.

    a. True
    b. False

3. What was one social movement in the 60s that used bluegrass as a "soundtrack"?

    a. Southern patriots
    b. Anti-consumerists
    c. Heroin legalizers
    d. All the above

4. What was the anthem of bluegrass's revival in the 60s?

    a. "O Death"
    b. "Blue Moon of Kentucky"
    c. "Man of Constant Sorrow"
    d. "Your Cheating Heart"

5. Bluegrass of the 60s had explicit political lyrics.

    a. True
    b. False

6. Sara Carter went back to performing in the 60s.

   a. True

   b. False

7. P. Carter toured with a separate band in the 60s.

   a. True

   b. False

8. Ricky Skaggs played with whom on stage as a child?

   a. Kitty Wells

   b. Bill Monroe

   c. Hank Williams

   d. None of the above

9. In the early 70s, Ricky Skaggs became an opening act for which of the following?

   a. Emmylou Harris

   b. The Rolling Stones

   c. Flat & Scruggs

   d. Clinch Mountain Boys

10. What was one country band that Ricky Skaggs and Emmylou Harris revived through renditions?

    a. Louvin Brothers

    b. Tammy Wynette's Quartet

    c. Ernest Tubb's Cowboys

    d. None of the above

11. In 70s country, it was a well-established formula to cover forgotten country songs.

a. True

b. False

12. Emmylou Harris and Ricky Skaggs attracted rock fans to country.

a. True

b. False

13. Which of the following artists followed in the footsteps of Emmylou Harris and Ricky Skaggs?

a. Loretta Lynn

b. Alison Krauss

c. Lita Ford

d. None of the above

14. Alison Krauss participated in the soundtrack of which movie?

a. The Outlaws

b. Highwaymen

c. Brother, Where Art Thou?

d. Top Gun

15. The bluegrass of the 70s reminded strongly of Bill Monroe.

a. True

b. False

16. Alison Krauss changed many record labels throughout her career.

a. True

b. False

17. Who was Gillian Welch's long-term musical partner?

a. Willie Nelson

b. Ricky Skaggs

c. David Rawlings

d. Brad Paisley

18. Which of the following songs is the "revenge of the Knoxville girl"?

a. "Caleb Meyer"

b. "Look at Miss Ohio"

c. "The Way It Goes"

d. None of the above

19. Gillian Welch had her own record label.

a. True

b. False

20. Alison Krauss never wanted to preserve traditional country; she was more inclined to rock.

a. True

b. False

QUIZ ANSWER KEY

1. False

2. True

3. Anti-consumerists

4. "Man of Constant Sorrow"

5. False

6. True

7. False

8. Bill Monroe

9. Clinch Mountain Boys

10. Louvin Brothers

11. False

12. True

13. Alison Krauss

14. Brother, Where Art Thou?

15. False

16. False

17. David Rawlings

18. "Caleb Meyer"

19. True

20. False

CHAPTER 12

THE MAN IN BLACK
AND THE PRISONER.

So, there were the pop country factories, the remaining honky tonkers, and the bluegrass gang. But there was one more important species in the mid-50s: those that destabilized Nashville from within. They were dressed in suits and sang country, but their lyrics were far from suburban fantasies. The most prominent member of this gang was Johnny Cash—The Man in Black. He was probably the first to play what we know as outlaw country today.

Johnny Cash was born into a poor cotton farmer family in Arkansas. He studied to become a radio announcer and played music at night, with his bandmates Luther Perkins and Marshal Grant. He eventually signed a record deal with Sam Phillips's Sun Records and was the first artist there to record a long-playing album. In other words, he had better privileges than early Elvis, who also recorded there.

Cash hit the charts in the 50s with "Folsom Prison Blues" (1957), "I Walk the Line" (1956), and "Home of Blues" (1957). Both country and rock audiences adored his deep voice and all-black attire. He soon got the nickname "the undertaker." In the early 60s, Cash toured with the Carter Family, which earned him a good reputation in the country music industry.

Eventually, in 1958, Johnny Cash made it to Columbia Records, Nashville. By that time, he was already addicted to multiple drugs and was beginning to get unstable. But that didn't stop him from being creative. Along the road to stardom, Cash shared an apartment with Waylon Jennings—another future legend—for a brief period of time.

While at Sun Records, Cash developed a unique sound. His guitarist, Luther Perkins, was a sloppy player, and Johnny would often get frustrated at that. But Sam Phillips loved Perkins's inability to play fluently. Phillips even banned Perkins from practicing, just so that the raw guitar sound could remain intact.

In Cash's band, there were no banjos, fiddles, or pianos. It was drums, bass, and acoustic guitar, plus deep singing. The popular saying "three chords and the truth" actually refers to Johnny Cash's early career.

Cash was also the new American cowboy: broad-shouldered, self-sufficient, black-clad, and spreading a message of redemption. He wore black as a protest against the wrongdoings in the world; but technically speaking, his artistic image was very much inspired by Gene Autry.

Undoubtedly, Johnny Cash's greatest feats were his live prison concerts. Playing live at prisons symbolized what Cash imagined as the revival of real country music: the transportation of country back to where it belonged—to the fallen, poor man, who suffers every day in his life. Cash reminded everyone, more and more of the deep roots of country music, which is why he was praised by a very large audience. Contrary to common belief, though, Cash himself has never been in prison.

He organized many prison concerts around the world, but one was of particular importance: *Johnny Cash at San Quentin* (1969). One prisoner at San Quentin was very amazed by Cash—by how he won the audience, how he mocked the guards, and how tough and straightforward he was. That prisoner saw a real business opportunity in singing before poor, working-class audiences. His name was Merle Haggard: this is the country boy who didn't just sing about being in prison, he'd been there.

Johnny Cash and Merle Haggard started performing together in the early 60s, and this is how Merle rose to fame. He was very authentic and immediately attracted country music fans. Young people were also interested in Merle's music until he released "Okie from Muskogee" (1969)—an anti-hippie song. In reality, Haggard had nothing against hippies. The song was meant to have a different connotation, something that only became clear years later.

QUIZ

1. Who is considered the first outlaw country singer?

   a. Ray Price
   b. Garth Brooks
   c. Johnny Cash
   d. Merle Haggard

2. The outlaws of country music destabilized Nashville from within.

   a. True
   b. False

3. Where was Johnny Cash born?

   a. New York
   b. Arkansas
   c. Texas
   d. All the above

4. In his early career, Johnny Cash signed with which label owned by Sam Phillips?

   a. Sony Records
   b. Columbia Records
   c. Sun Records
   d. Motown Records

5. Sam Phillips produced another prominent American musician simultaneously with Johnny Cash. Who was he?

a. Merle Haggard

b. Elvis Presley

c. Johnny Mitchell

d. None of the above

6. In his early career, Johnny Cash was allowed to record a long-playing album, while other musicians weren't.

a. True

b. False

7. In the early 60s, Johnny Cash toured with the Carter Family.

a. True

b. False

8. When was "Folsom Prison Blues" by Johnny Cash released?

a. 1957

b. 1961

c. 1966

d. 1970

9. Which of the following is one of Johnny Cash's early hits?

a. "Hurt"

b. "Bridge Over Troubled Water"

c. "God's Gonna Cut You Down"

d. "I Walk the Like"

10. During his early career, Johnny Cash shared an apartment with which country musician?

a. Waylon Jennings

b. Merle Haggard

c. Tompall Glaser

d. Willie Nelson

11. By the time he signed with Columbia Records, Johnny Cash had already given up drugs.

    a. True

    b. False

12. Sam Phillips didn't allow Cash's guitarist Luther Perkins to practice, because he liked Perkins's lack of technical guitar skills.

    a. True

    b. False

13. Which of the following instruments was not featured in Johnny Cash's early recordings?

    a. Acoustic guitar

    b. Banjo

    c. Drums

    d. Bass

14. Who was the primary inspiration behind Johnny Cash's all-black attire?

    a. Gene Autry

    b. Hawkshaw Hawkins

    c. Buddy Holly

    d. Robert Johnson

15. Where did Johnny Cash meet Merle Haggard?

    a. Arkansas

    b. Columbia Records

    c. San Quentin Prison

    d. Folsom Prison

16. Johnny Cash spent ten years in prison before he became a country star.

    a. True

    b. False

17. Merle Haggard initially became popular through performing with Johnny Cash.

    a. True

    b. False

18. Which of the following was written by Merle Haggard?

    a. "Give My Love to Rose"

    b. "Folsom Prison Blues"

    c. "Okie from Muskogee"

    d. None of the above

19. The phrase "three chords and the truth" stems from Johnny Cash's early career.

    a. True

    b. False

20. Johnny Cash studied to become a radio announcer before rising as a country music star.

    a. True

    b. False

QUIZ ANSWER KEY

1. Johnny Cash

2. True

3. Arkansas

4. Sun Records

5. Elvis Presley

6. True

7. True

8. 1957

9. "I Walk the Like"

10. Waylon Jennings

11. False

12. True

13. Banjo

14. Gene Autry

15. San Quentin Prison

16. False

17. True

18. "Okie from Muskogee"

19. True

20. True

CHAPTER 13

THE OUTLAWS.

There was a janitor at Columbia Records who was very fond of Johnny Cash. He never stopped terrorizing the big man with song ideas. And Johnny was interested in this janitor's music. The janitor was Kris Kristofferson. Most of his song ideas got rejected, until "Sunday Morning Coming Down" in 1969.

Kris Kristofferson was a poor kid, who had lost his family, and was not doing much with his life, except for saving up for dope and alcohol. He had the time of his life when Cash sang one of his hangover songs. Yet, in the eyes of country musicians, the release of "Sunday Morning" was a much more serious moment in history. The ultimate American hero—Johnny Cash—was singing about smoking and drinking. That immediately opened the doors for country outlaws, who had been hiding in the shadows.

Kris became more popular than Merle Haggard, and his stoned appearance at the awards in 1970 gave him a serious dose of publicity. For the first time, a kid dared to disrespect the institution of the Country Music Awards. Although Kris was not stoned that night, he might have been drunk.

According to Willie Nelson, Kris Kristofferson came right when country music needed him. The outlaws—tough, non-conforming, raw country singers—were now free to demolish the fake Nashville industry. The liberal youth labeled these outlaws as rednecks, but nothing could stop the new wave of country from hitting hard.

There was one singer who caused a great deal of confusion among critics. Charlie Pride was an African American who sang traditional country and was inspired by Hank Williams. Some people found it hard to digest that a Black man was singing the white man's blues. Pride remains the most successful African American country musician to this day.

The political climate was tough. Tensions grew between the patriots and the radical liberals, and the voice of the common man was stifled. This is where Merle Haggard stepped in with "Okie from Muscogee." He did not write the song against anyone. He wrote it *for* the common man, who was forgotten by the media and overlooked by the intellectuals.

The outlaw movement culminated with the album *Wanted! The Outlaws* in 1976. The album was a compilation of songs by Willie Nelson, Waylon Jennings, Jessie Colter (Waylon's wife, a successful solo singer), and Tompall Glaser (owner of the legendary Nashville recording studio Hillbilly Central).

The outlaws wore cowboy hats and beards. This is what the country look would be from then on, for at least 30 years. They not only drank whisky but also smoked pot. They inspired a new genre of cowboy movies: the cowboy was not an assistant to the sheriff but a complete outlaw who protected the poor and downtrodden. These outlaws served as the biggest influences on future rock stars—such as Keith Richards and Ringo Starr.

In the early 70s, Nashville's plans to merge country and pop were beginning to fail. Willie Nelson had spent most of the 60s there and he wrote some great songs. But the producers usually used those songs for other singers' repertoires. Willie didn't have much success as a recording artist. Yet, his ideas were much bigger than those of Nashville.

Willie got his band together and moved to his hometown of Austin, Texas. They started playing at Armadillo World Headquarters, a counterculture hotspot that was full of young people. This is where Willie brought rednecks and hippies together. Young people began to realize that the outlaws were on their side, and that there was no reason for tensions. Before that, the audience had been split in two by barriers.

QUIZ

1. Where was Kris Kristofferson working as a janitor when he met Johnny Cash?

   a. Sam's Place

   b. Armadillo World Headquarters

   c. Columbia Records

   d. Sun Records

2. Johnny Cash was not at all interested in Kris Kristofferson's early song ideas.

   a. True

   b. False

3. In what year did Johnny Cash record Kris Kristofferson's "Sunday Morning"?

   a. 1965

   b. 2002

   c. 1969

   d. 1971

4. "Sunday Morning Coming Down" brought gospel lyrics back into country music.

   a. True

   b. False

5. In what year did Kris Kristofferson receive an award for "Sunday Morning"?

a. 2010

b. 1975

c. 1968

d. 1970

6. Kris Kristofferson had a poor life before becoming a country star.

   a. True

   b. False

7. Kris Kristofferson was heavily stoned when he received his award for "Sunday Morning."

   a. True

   b. False

8. The outlaws were labeled as rednecks by which political group?

   a. Patriots

   b. Liberal youth

   c. Conservative youth

   d. They were never labeled as rednecks

9. Who was Charlie Pride's main musical inspiration?

   a. Bob Seger

   b. Aretha Franklin

   c. Merle Haggard

   d. Hank Williams

10. Political intellectuals of the 60s quickly embraced the image of Charlie Pride.

   a. True

   b. False

11. Charlie Pride is the most successful African American country singer of all time.

    a. True

    b. False

12. Which of the following country songs caused a serious political uproar in the 60s?

    a. "Honky Tonk Heroes"

    b. "Okie from Muscogee"

    c. "Folsom Prison Blues"

    d. "Slipping Around"

13. Merle Haggard was an anti-hippie activist.

    a. True

    b. False

14. Which of the following artists was featured in the album *Wanted! The Outlaws*?

    a. Charlie Pride

    b. Merle Haggard

    c. Tompall Glaser

    d. Johnny Cash

15. In what year was *Wanted! The Outlaws* released?

    a. 1981

    b. 1966

    c. 1976

    d. 1961

16. The outlaws were clean-shaven cowboys, who protested against drugs and alcohol.

a. True

b. False

17. Rock and roll stars were also inspired by the outlaw country look.

a. True

b. False

18. In which Texas venue did Willie Nelson start playing after he left Nashville?

a. Armadillo World Headquarters

b. Dallas Cowboy Shack

c. Houston Hills

d. Sam's Place

19. When Willie Nelson came to Texas, the club audience was split into hippies and rednecks.

a. True

b. False

20. In his early Nashville years, Willie Nelson was a successful recording artist.

a. True

b. False

QUIZ ANSWER KEY

1. Columbia Records

2. False

3. 1969

4. False

5. 1970

6. True

7. True

8. Liberal youth

9. Hank Williams

10. 40s popular music

11. True

12. "Okie from Muscogee"

13. False

14. Tompall Glaser

15. 1976

16. False

17. True

18. Armadillo World Headquarters

19. True

20. False

CHAPTER 14

THE DEMISE OF NASHVILLE.

Willie Nelson imagined music in a much purer way than did Nashville. His idea was to get his band in the studio and record albums on the spot. When producers heard these recordings, they thought they were listening to demos. Little did they know that Willie Nelson's albums *Phases and Stages* (1972), *Shotgun Willie* (1973), and *Red Headed Stranger* (1975) would set the ultimate standard for country music sound.

Willie Nelson unleashed the siege against Nashville, but he wasn't the first. Bakersfield, CA, had Buck Owens as a weapon of its own since the 50s. Buck was a honky tonker who relied on impulsive and raw performance, with twangy electric guitars and loud, energetic arrangements. Nashville mocked the Bakersfield sound, but radio stations loved it. The 70s were the perfect time for it to rise back to fame.

Behind the Bakersfield sound was producer Ken Nelson. He had a hands-off approach to recording, which allowed Owens to fully develop his musical ideas. Buck's "Act Naturally" (1963) was covered by The Beatles in 1965. Ironically, though, the Bakersfield sound was produced at Capitol Records, Hollywood.

Historically, the outlaw movement came from Oklahoma immigrants, after the Dust Bowl of the 30s. These were poor working people, and most of them never really got out of poverty. In the late 60s, Merle Haggard was their hero. "Working Man Blues" (1969) and "Mama's Hungry Eyes" (1969) describe the poor life and the reasons behind the outlaw movement.

Merle Haggard was also the primary inspiration for Californian legend Gram Parsons. Gram and his band The Flying Burrito Brothers were the early pioneers of country rock. That movement went on for many years after that, with Linda Ronstadt, The Eagles, Fleetwood Mac, and many others.

Gram Parsons himself was another huge influence on Emmylou Harris. They did some spontaneous duets in the 70s, and she claims that it was Gram who introduced her to the emotional depths of country music. Parsons died of an overdose in 1973. A weird funeral followed, where they burned him at the Joshua Tree National Park, CA. Emmylou's "Boulder to Birmingham" (1975) is dedicated to Gram's death.

Nashville was attacked from all sides in the 1970s. The feudal producers had no choice but to adapt. Even artists from within the establishment demanded change. But the man who caused the most damage was Waylon Jennings. He was an ex-bassist for Buddy Holly, rock and roller, honky tonker, and a gun-toting outlaw. In 1959, he gave up his seat on the plane that killed Buddy Holly.

As you can hear in "Are You Sure Hank Done It This Way" (1975), Waylon was an enemy of the Nashville system. He was a free-spirited Texan, with tough-looking friends and customers. It took some nerve to get to him. Yet, one songwriter made it through— Billy Joe Shaver. Shaver's "Honky Tonk Heroes" helped Waylon to rise to the top of country charts.

The other thing Waylon needed was an independent studio. That was provided to him by Tompall Glaser—"Hillbilly Central" in Nashville. The schedule was chaotic, and there was plenty of booze at the sessions, which was great for Waylon.

The outlaws had the music, the looks, and the attitude, but they never were an organized movement. Nashville released the 1976 album not because they approved of the rebellion, but because they noticed young people wearing cowboy hats with feathers. Nashville sensed an opportunity for a new cowboy trend. A whole new fashion industry started with the outlaws. And you did not necessarily have to listen to country to dress like an outlaw.

QUIZ

1. Which of the following is a full album by Willie Nelson?

   a. Phases and Stages

   b. The Man Comes Around

   c. Wanted! The Outlaws

   d. Interiors

2. Nashville producers in the 60s thought that Willie Nelson's albums were demo recordings.

   a. True

   b. False

3. Which genre of alt country did Buck Owens develop?

   a. Punk country

   b. Bakersfield sound

   c. Texas honky tonk

   d. None of the above

4. Nashville producers were impressed by Buck Owens's alternative country sound.

   a. True

   b. False

5. Who was the producer behind Buck Owens's success?

   a. Chet Atkins

   b. Phil Spector

   c. Sam Phillips

   d. Ken Nelson

6. The outlaw movement started with Oklahoma immigrants, after the Dust Bowl.

    a. True

    b. False

7. "Mama's Hungry Eyes" is a song by Willie Nelson.

    a. True

    b. False

8. Who is often considered the hero of 60s country music outlaws?

    a. Merle Haggard

    b. Garth Brooks

    c. Hank Williams

    d. Bruce Springsteen

9. Which of the following songs was written by Buck Owens and covered by The Beatles?

    a. "Honky Tonk Heroes"

    b. "Heartaches by the Number"

    c. "Act Naturally"

    d. "I Wanna Be Your Man"

10. Which of the following bands were early pioneers of country rock?

    a. The Highwaymen

    b. The Monkees

    c. The Flying Burrito Brothers

    d. The Eagles

11. Gram Parsons was strongly inspired by Merle Haggard.

    a. True

    b. False

12. Alt country artists rebelled against Nashville, but artists from within the system never did.

    a. True

    b. False

13. Gram Parsons famously recorded country duets with which female singer?

    a. Janis Joplin

    b. Emmylou Harris

    c. Loretta Lynn

    d. Tammy Wynette

14. Which of the following songs was dedicated to Gram Parson's death?

    a. "He Stopped Loving Her Today"

    b. "Stand by Your Man"

    c. "Boulder to Birmingham"

    d. "Piece of My Heart"

15. Before moving on to a solo country career, Waylon Jennings played bass for whom?

    a. The Rolling Stones

    b. Bill Monroe

    c. Buddy Holly

    d. None of the above

16. Waylon Jennings was a tough, gun-toting cowboy from Texas.

    a. True
    b. False

17. Which of the following songs was written by Billy Joe Shaver and performed by Waylon Jennings?

    a. "Are You Sure Hank Done It This Way"
    b. "Honky Tonk Heroes (Like Me)"
    c. "Live Forever"
    d. None of the above

18. What was the name of the studio, owned by Tompall Glaser, where Waylon Jennings recorded?

    a. Hillbilly Central
    b. Nashville's Dearest
    c. Armadillo Headquarters
    d. Glaser's Hut

19. In the 70s, Nashville perceived the outlaw country movement as a fashion trend.

    a. True
    b. False

20. Despite the outlaws in the early 70s, Nashville's production-line pop country was more popular than ever.

    a. True
    b. False

QUIZ ANSWER KEY

1. Phases and Stages

2. True

3. Bakersfield sound

4. False

5. Ken Nelson

6. True

7. False

8. Merle Haggard

9. "Act Naturally"

10. The Flying Burrito Brothers

11. True

12. False

13. Emmylou Harris

14. "Boulder to Birmingham"

15. Buddy Holly

16. True

17. "Honky Tonk Heroes"

18. "Hillbilly Central"

19. 1950s

20. False

CHAPTER 15

A STEP TOWARDS
THE MODERN AGE.

A wise man once said, "Authenticity is only an issue when you don't have it." In the late 70s, authenticity was once again leaving country music. Everyone looked like an outlaw, but no one cared to understand outlaw music. This was the fight that country musicians like Dwight Yoakam had to fight for most of their lives. Dwight played hardcore country, heavily inspired by Buck Owens. He didn't have to pretend to be an outlaw, but the 80s rejected his music as old fashioned.

The other two notable young countrymen were Randy Travis and Steve Earle. Randy was a skilled singer, who lured his audience into George Jones's and other dinosaurs' music. Steve did entirely original material, inspired by both country classics and American rock. Those three are known in country music history as the New Traditionalists. They were rejected for a long time, but their turn did come when authenticity became an issue.

The New Traditionalists adapted country music to contemporary audiences, much like Alison Kraus did. Also, Steve was happy to continue into the direction of original music—his unbounded country rock. Country fans loved him, but others saw a bigger opportunity there. In 1989, Garth Brooks stepped on the stairs Steve had built and launched the largest country music product of the century. He toured the country with ten-ton trucks and delivered the most amazing live shows. This is when commercial country finally gained momentum and established itself as a separate, intact genre.

Garth was no stranger. He was a highly-skilled singer and a marketing graduate. He knew what he was doing and how to do it. He was also one of the few people to receive a standing ovation at the Bluebird Café in Nashville, where he was discovered.

Country fans had no problem with Garth, except that he attracted huge audiences who never had—nor ever would—listen to classic country. Garth's fans were amused by the light shows and the sounds, and many never did explore country music beyond Brooks. He sold around 50 million records, and at one point, was second only to The Beatles.

Nashville fell in love with Garth's formula and decided to take on a new strategy: invest in just a handful of artists, make records quickly, focus on videos and live shows, and forget all the old stuff.

MTV also hit country music. Suddenly, half-naked females were singing country music, and Nashville, the old home of the *Opry*, was behind it all. And it was not only the producers. The artists themselves—for example, Shania Twain and Faith Hill—sensed the opportunity to sell their own attractiveness.

But as you might have noticed already, music history moves in cycles. Soon enough, the need for authenticity arose again. The 1990s and 2000s gave birth to plenty of alt country artists, such as

Wilco and Ryan Adams. Randy Travis continued his career successfully. The new alt country had a mixed heritage of rock, country, and punk, but fans in the 90s had no problem with that. These artists were supported by their communities, even though country radio never allowed their songs to be played.

Another significant event of the 2000s was the return of Johnny Cash with *American III: Solitary Man* (2000) and *American IV: The Man Comes Around* (2002). The albums contain both original Cash songs and covers of selected songs of all genres. This is where the famous Cash version of the Nine Inch Nails song "Hurt" comes from.

It was amazing how 90s youth embraced traditional and outlaw country. Even today, you can see kids on the street wearing Cash and Hank Williams t-shirts. Also, the fact that Hank Williams III is enjoying a successful career means that authenticity is back in demand.

QUIZ

1. Which of the following musicians was a New Traditionalist?

    a. Steve Earle

    b. Johnny Cash

    c. Hawkshaw Hawkins

    d. Elvis Presley

2. In the late 70s, country music once again lacked authenticity.

    a. True

    b. False

3. Steve Earl's original music laid the foundation for which artist?

    a. Buck Owens

    b. Garth Brooks

    c. Gram Parsons

    d. All the above

4. When was the most recent wave of authentic country?

    a. Late 50s

    b. Late 60s

    c. Late 70s

    d. Late 90s

5. Which of the following artists played alt country?

    a. Bryan Adams

    b. Ryan Adams

    c. Kurt Cobain

    d. Kid Rock

6. Dwight Yoakam switched to commercial country in the 80s.

   a. True

   b. False

7. Country music never made it to MTV.

   a. True

   b. False

8. Which genre influenced 90s alt country?

   a. Jazz

   b. Vaudeville

   c. Punk

   d. Flamenco

9. Which of these is a 21st-century comeback album by Johnny Cash?

   a. Train Songs

   b. Live at Folsom Prison II

   c. I Walk the Line

   d. American IV: The Man Comes Around

10. Female country artists were forced to show nudity in the late 80s?

   a. True

   b. False

11. At one point, Garth Brooks was second only to The Beatles on the charts.

   a. True

   b. False

12. Garth Brooks' fans were committed to traditional country.

    a. True

    b. False

13. Where was Garth Brooks discovered?

    a. Hard Rock Café, Dallas

    b. Rainbow, Los Angeles

    c. Bluebird Café, Nashville

    d. Sam's Place, Bakersfield

14. Garth Brooks amused his audiences with what?

    a. Old country music

    b. Hank Williams covers

    c. Carter Family covers

    d. Stage light and sound

15. What formula did Nashville adopt following Garth Brooks's success?

    a. Invest only in male artists

    b. Invest in a few artists and focus on videos

    c. Go back to the honky tonk look

    d. Dress everyone in black, like Johnny Cash

16. Garth Brooks delivered simple, one-man acoustic performances.

    a. True

    b. False

17. What education did Garth Brooks have?

    a. Jazz Trumpet

    b. Engineering

c. Marketing

d. Classical Music

18. Who wrote the original version of the ballad "Hurt"?

a. Johnny Cash

b. Alison Krauss

c. Nine Inch Nails

d. Hank Williams

19. Hank Williams's grandchildren are not musicians.

a. True

b. False

20. In the 21st century, the interest in authentic country has vanished.

a. True

b. False

QUIZ ANSWER KEY

1. Steve Earle

2. True

3. Garth Brooks

4. Late 90s

5. Ryan Adams

6. False

7. False

8. Punk

9. American IV: The Man Comes Around

10. False

11. True

12. False

13. Bluebird Café, Nashville

14. Stage light and sound

15. Invest in a few artists and focus on videos

16. False

17. Marketing

18. Nine Inch Nails

19. False

20. False

CHAPTER 16

WOMEN IN COUNTRY MUSIC.

Country music also served as a platform for women's independence in the 20th century. It all started with Sara Carter and Patsy Montana. Sara was a divorced wife, who smoked and wore slacks— quite a revolutionary look at the time. Patsy's "I Want to Be a Cowboy's Sweetheart" (1935) was also a scandal. No one before her had dared sing about doing what men did! You either had to be the cowgirl or nothing.

During WWII, women went into the factories and earned financial independence. That soon reflected in country music. In 1952, desperate singer Kitty Wells was about to give up singing when she was offered a $30 session gig. She went on to record one of the biggest hits ever, "It Wasn't God Who Made Honky Tonk Angels," a response to Hank Thompson's "Wild Side of Life" (1952).

From there on out, women too could be honky tonkers. Yet, the industry establishment was not okay with that. Radio stations never played two female records back to back; it was hard for new artists. One notable tough girl was Jean Shepard. Born in a poor Oklahoma family, her father pawned all their furniture so that teenage Jean could buy an upright bass. She had to make it, and she did. Her "A Dear John Letter" (1953) was the first female country record to sell more than a million copies.

Jean won the audience by challenging male attitudes—something no one had previously considered a successful formula. But 10 million copies sold, producers began to rethink. Then came hardened honky tonker, Patsy Cline. Patsy introduced emotion to hillbilly music; check out her cover of Nelson's "Crazy" (1961). She died in a plane crash in 1963, together with Shepard's husband Hawkshaw Hawkins.

The 60s saw three standard-setting women: Loretta Lynn, Tammy Wynette, and Dolly Parton. Loretta was the hillbilly feminist. She was bold in the songs she wrote; check out "The Pill" (1975). Similarly, Wynette had a rocky life, divorced three times, and sang plenty of controversial songs, the most notable being "Stand by Your Man" (1968).

Then there was Dolly Parton with her "Dumb Blonde" in 1966. Dolly was different in that she exposed her sexiness and was way more extravagant. In 1967, she became the girl singer for *The Porter Wagoner Show*, then started a solo career, and then rose to international fame. These three women recorded the legendary album *Honky Tonk Angels* in 1993.

In the 80s, Parton headed to LA to pursue a movie career. Meanwhile, one of the many women she inspired released the hit "Seven Year Ache" (1981). Her name was Rosanne and she was the daughter of Johnny Cash. Rosanne drew from country, rock, blues, and Americana. It was Rosanne who broke the lyrical barrier in country music. She opened the doors for poetry.

Despite the many female successes, though, the Nashville male establishment hadn't changed their attitude much since the 50s. The woman who challenged these men in the 80s was Gail Davies, the first female producer in country. She is best known for her provocative cover of Tammy Wynette's "Unwed Fathers" (1984).

Another surprise for 80s country was gay female singer k.d. lang. Despite her sexuality and punk vibe, though, true country fans embraced her as their own. Check out "Honky Tonk Angels Medley" (1988), where she sings with Loretta Lynn, Kitty Wells, and Brenda Lee.

Yet the biggest shock came in the 90s with Shania Twain—a singer so outrageous that her videos were denied at first. She went on a famous shopping mall tour to promote herself. This is when MTV noticed her and made her an international star within a few months. Shania was the founder of the sexy female movement in country that we still know today.

QUIZ

1. Who was the first woman in country to sell more than a million records?

   a. Dolly Parton

   b. Patsy Cline

   c. Jean Shepard

   d. Shania Twain

2. Patsy Montana was a regular cowgirl.

   a. True

   b. False

3. Jean Shepard's lyrics challenged what?

   a. Political leaders

   b. Male attitudes

   c. Female attitudes

   d. All the above

4. "The Pill" was written by whom?

   a. Kitty Wells

   b. Loretta Lynn

   c. Tammy Wynette

   d. Patsy Montana

5. Who was the next big 80s star after Dolly Parton started her movie career?

   a. Gillian Welch

   b. Tammy Wynette

c. Shania Twain

d. Rosanne Cash

6. The Nashville establishment was against women being honky tonkers.

   a. True

   b. False

7. Sara Carter remained a typical Victorian girl after she rose to fame.

   a. True

   b. False

8. Which of the following songs was written by Rosanne Cash?

   a. "Seven Year Ache"

   b. "A Dear John Letter"

   c. "The Pill"

   d. "Unwed Fathers"

9. Kitty Wells wrote which of the following?

   a. "The Pill"

   b. "A Dear John Letter"

   c. "Crazy"

   d. "It Wasn't God Who Made Honky Tonk Angels"

10. Which of the following describes young Dolly Parton?

   a. Extravagance

   b. Humility

   c. Punk

   d. Vaudeville

11. Jean Shepard was born in a rich, aristocratic family.

    a. True

    b. False

12. Patsy Cline introduced emotional singing to country music.

    a. True

    b. False

13. Who else was in the plane where Patsy Cline died?

    a. P. Carter

    b. Hawkshaw Hawkins

    c. Buddy Holly

    d. Jean Shepard

14. "It Wasn't God Who Made Honky Tonk Angels" was a response to which of the following?

    a. Hank Williams's "Your Cheating Heart"

    b. Johnny Cash's "I Walk the Line"

    c. Hank Thompson's "Wild Side of Life"

    d. Patsy Montana's "I Want to Be A Cowboy's Sweetheart"

15. Which of the following women was the first female producer in country music?

    a. Loretta Lynn

    b. Dolly Parton

    c. Gail Davies

    d. Faith Hill

16. Tammy Wynette was against feminist country.

    a. True

    b. False

17. Dolly Parton's first hit was which one?

    a. "Coat of Many Colors"

    b. "Jolene"

    c. "Dumb Blonde"

    d. "Islands in the Stream"

18. Country audiences resented k.d. lang because of her sexuality?

    a. True

    b. False

19. When did Dolly Parton join *The Porter Wagoner Show*?

    a. 1967

    b. 1952

    c. 1969

    d. 1970

20. The aftermath of WWII demotivated women to make music.

    a. True

    b. False

QUIZ ANSWER KEY

1. Jean Shepard

2. False

3. Male attitudes

4. Loretta Lynn

5. Rosanne Cash

6. True

7. False

8. "Seven Year Ache"

9. "It Wasn't God Who Made Honky Tonk Angels"

10. Extravagance

11. False

12. True

13. Hawkshaw Hawkins

14. Hank Thompson's "Wild Side of Life"

15. Gail Davies

16. False

17. "Dumb Blonde"

18. False

19. 1967

20. False

CHAPTER 17

KRIS KRISTOFFERSON.

Let's go back to the roots of outlaw country. We left off where Kris Kristofferson wrote "Sunday Morning Coming Down" for Johnny Cash in 1969 and received an award in 1970. There is, however, more history worth sharing about this emblematic country artist. Did you know that he also wrote Janis Joplin's "Me and Bobby McGee"? And also Bill Nash's "For the Good Times"?

When Kris was a child, his father pushed him to become a military man. Along the way, however, Kris enrolled in college in California and became a popular writer. He was also a skilled athlete. In the late 50s, he received an Oxford scholarship and graduated (English Literature) in 1960. As you can see, Johnny Cash's janitor was no stranger to art and literature.

Yet, Kris did try the military life for a while. In the early 60s, he became a Captain and was stationed in West Germany. At that time Kris started playing and writing music more seriously. He was so serious about music that he left the army in 1965. This decision led to his family disowning him. But despite all that, Kris earned the Veteran of the Year Award in 2003.

After leaving the military, Kris went to Nashville to look for opportunities. Life was hard there, and his son was sick. On top of that, he divorced his wife. This is how he ended up sweeping floors at Columbia Records and meeting Johnny Cash. But there was one more important period before that. Before Nashville, Kris was a commercial helicopter pilot in Louisiana. He claims that he wrote "Bobby McGee" and "Help Me Make It Through the Night" during these pilot years.

But how exactly did Kris Kristofferson gain Johnny Cash's attention in 1969? He landed a helicopter in Cash's front yard and gave him "Sunday Morning." This is no joke!

Before "Sunday Morning," Kris had already begun some sort of a music career. In 1966, Dave Dudley released Kristofferson's "Viet Nam Blues." In 1967, Kris became a songwriter for Epic Records. In the following decades, a multitude of artists released songs written by him: Waylon Jennings, Ray Price, Jerry Lee Lewis, and Ray Stevens, just to name a few.

After Epic Records, Kris decided to try a career as a performer himself. He joined Monument Records and released *Kristofferson* in 1970. That was not a very successful album. Yet, the demand for Kris's songwriting grew even stronger. His second album *The Silver Tongued Devil and I* (1971) did sell quite well. It included the evergreen "Loving Her Was Easier." The industry finally then accepted Kris as a fully able performer and songwriter.

Quick fact: Kris Kristofferson dated Janis Joplin in the late 60s. So, "Me and Bobby McGee" is no big coincidence.

In the mid-70s, Kris Kristofferson started a movie career. In 1976, he received a Best Actor Golden Globe Award for the movie *A Star is Born*—the one from 1976, of course, not the new one! Meanwhile, in 1973, Kris released the hit album *Full Moon*, together with his new wife Rita Coolidge. Nevertheless, his next album *Spooky Lady's Sideshow* was a failure and set his remaining career as a performer on a downward trend.

In 1985, Kris Kristofferson, Willie Nelson, Waylon Jennings, and Johnny Cash formed the super-group The Highwaymen. The band's first album *Highwayman* (1985) was successful, but they did not have much success in the 90s. In 1995, they stopped recording. For the rest of his career, Kris continued to receive numerous awards for his songwriting talent. In 2004, he was inducted to the Country Music Hall of Fame.

QUIZ

1. Which of the following artists had a hit in 1971 that was written by Kris Kristofferson?

    a. Jimi Hendrix

    b. Janis Joplin

    c. Jean Shepard

    d. Shania Twain

2. Kris Kristofferson wrote Bill Nash's "For the Good Times."

    a. True

    b. False

3. In college, Kris Kristofferson focused on what activities?

    a. Politics and sociology

    b. Writing and sports

    c. Engineering and mathematics

    d. None of the above

4. What was Kris Kristofferson's college education?

    a. Swedish Literature

    b. Music Theory

    c. English Literature

    d. Mechanical Engineering

5. Where was Kris Kristofferson stationed as a soldier?

    a. East Germany

    b. USSR

c. Vietnam

d. West Germany

6. During his soldier years, Kris Kristofferson left songwriting and music behind.

   a. True

   b. False

7. Kris Kristofferson knew Johnny Cash from his teenage years.

   a. True

   b. False

8. In 1966, Dave Dudley released which song written by Kris Kristofferson?

   a. "Viet Nam Blues"

   b. "Six Days on the Road"

   c. "Me and ol' C.B."

   d. "Lovesick Blues"

9. In 1967, Kris Kristofferson became a songwriter for which label?

   a. Columbia Records

   b. Epic Records

   c. Sun Records

   d. Chess Records

10. Which of the following artists has not released songs by Kris Kristofferson?

    a. Hawkshaw Hawkins

    b. Waylon Jennings

    c. Ray Price

    d. Jerry Lee Lewis

11. Kris Kristofferson wrote some of his greatest hits while he was a pilot in the 60s.

    a. True

    b. False

12. Kris Kristofferson landed a helicopter in Johnny Cash's front yard to get attention.

    a. True

    b. False

13. What was Kris Kristofferson's first studio album as a performer?

    a. The Last Movie

    b. Kristofferson

    c. The Silver Tongued Devil and I

    d. The Old Grey Whistle Test

14. Which of the following songs was on the album *The Silver Tongued Devil and I*?

    a. "Me and Bobby McGee"

    b. "I'd Rather Be Sorry"

    c. "Loving Her Was Easier"

    d. "I've Got to Have You"

15. For which movie did Kris Kristofferson receive a Golden Globe Award?

    a. Hanover Street

    b. Convoy

    c. A Star is Born

    d. Blume in Love

16. Kris Kristofferson dated Janis Joplin in the late 60s.

a. True

b. False

17. Which album set the beginning of Kris Kristofferson's downturn as a performer?

a. Full Moon

b. Spooky Lady's Sideshow

c. Kristofferson

d. The Silver Tongued Devil and I

18. The Highwaymen recorded until 2005.

a. True

b. False

19. When did Kris Kristofferson release *The Silver Tongued Devil and I*?

a. 1980

b. 1975

c. 1971

d. 1969

20. Kris Kristofferson's family disowned him because he left the military.

a. True

b. False

QUIZ ANSWER KEY

1. Janis Joplin

2. True

3. Writing and sports

4. English Literature

5. West Germany

6. False

7. False

8. "Viet Nam Blues"

9. Epic Records

10. Hawkshaw Hawkins

11. True

12. True

13. Kristofferson

14. "Loving Her Was Easier"

15. A Star is Born

16. True

17. Spooky Lady's Sideshow

18. False

19. 1971

20. True

CHAPTER 18

KENNY ROGERS.

Some years after Hank Williams's death, another remarkable country star began his career: Kenny Rogers. In the late 50s, Kenny started by playing rock and roll and psychedelic rock. He had a small hit in 1957 ("That Crazy Feeling"), but his career didn't really take off, so he joined the jazz band Bobby Doyle Three. In 1966, the band broke apart, after their single "Here's That Rainy Day" was a commercial failure.

Meanwhile, Kenny had been developing his songwriting and production abilities. He was also a session musician for Eddy Arnold. Having gained some reputation in the industry, Kenny was accepted as a singer and double bass player for the New Christy Minstrels in 1966. That band, however, didn't offer him much opportunity, so he took some members from it and established The First Edition in 1967.

For the next ten years, The First Edition released a string of singles, which hit both country and pop charts. But they did not necessarily stick to traditional country. One of these hits was "Just Dropped In" (1968), which you may know from *The Big Lebowski*. Kenny Rogers played bass and sang lead vocals on that song.

The First Edition broke up in 1976, and Kenny began an astounding solo career. He signed with United Artists and released the album *Love Lifted Me*—which contained the song "Runaway Girl," featured in *Trackdown* (1976). Later that same year (1976), Kenny released his second solo album *Kenny Rogers*, where you can find the mega hit "Laura."

Using the momentum, Kenny released the single "Lucille" (1977), which took him to a whole new level in country music. A massively up-trending era in his career followed, with *The Gambler* in 1978 and "Coward of the County" in 1979. Kenny achieved all this success with the help of producer Larry Butler; their partnership ended in 1980.

During and after the Larry Butler era, Kenny Rogers recorded golden hits with Dottie West, Kim Carnes, Lynda Carter, and others. One of these hits was "Every Time Two Fools Collide" (1978). These duets cemented Kenny's name in the country music industry, and in 1980, he partnered with Lionel Richie to release "Lady." For the rest of the 80s, Rogers released a long series of hit albums and singles.

And he didn't stop there. In 1981, Kenny bought ABC Dunhill's old building in LA and built one of the most advanced recording studios in the world to this day. Part of "We Are the World" was recorded in that studio.

In 1983, Kenny Rogers went on to work with Barry Gibb of Bee Gees. They released the album *Eyes That See in the Dark*, featuring "Islands in the Stream"—Kenny's legendary duet with Dolly Parton. Bee Gees originally wrote "Islands in the Stream" for Marvin Gaye, but quickly switched to Kenny Rogers once they heard his version.

In 1988, Kenny Rogers received a Grammy Award for Best Country

Collaboration with Vocals for his duet with Ronnie Milsap, "Make no Mistake, She's Mine." Many other mega-hits and collaborations followed. In 1992, Kenny became co-owner and headliner of Grand Palace Theater in Boston, Missouri. In 1994, he released *Timepiece*, an album of jazz standards that Kenny had performed with Bobby Doyle Three back in the day.

All in all, Kenny Rogers released more than 60 top singles, which were included in both country and pop charts through the years. To this day, Kenny is remembered as one of the most successful country music writers, performers, and producers. In 2015, he announced his farewell tour—*The Gambler's Last Deal*—and passed away in March 2020. One little known fact is that, despite his huge success and numerous connections, Kenny Rogers kept the same session band, Bloodline, since 1976.

QUIZ

1. What was Kenny Rogers's first small hit in 1957?

    a. "Loving Her Was Easier"

    b. "The Gambler"

    c. "That Crazy Feeling"

    d. "Here's That Rainy Day"

2. Kenny Rogers started playing country and bluegrass music in the 50s.

    a. True

    b. False

3. In the late 50s, Kenny Rogers joined which jazz band?

    a. Dave Brubeck's Quintet

    b. Miles Davis's Quintet

    c. Bobby Doyle Three

    d. John Coltrane's Trio

4. Which song put an end to Kenny Rogers's early jazz career?

    a. "Bitches Brew"

    b. "Here's That Rainy Day"

    c. "That Crazy Feeling"

    d. "Living Alone"

5. In 1966, Kenny Rogers became the double bass player for which band?

    a. The Flying Burritos

    b. Ralph Stanley's Trio

c. Bill Haley and His Comets

d. New Christy Minstrels

6. 1967's The First Edition consisted of musicians taken from the band in the previous question.

   a. True

   b. False

7. The First Edition played strictly bluegrass and old country.

   a. True

   b. False

8. In the early 60s, Kenny Rogers was a session musician for whom?

   a. Eddie Arnold

   b. Phil Spector

   c. Bill Haley

   d. Frank Sinatra

9. Which song by The First Edition was featured in *The Big Lebowski*?

   a. "Ruby, Don't Take Your Love to Town"

   b. "But You Know I Love You"

   c. "The Gambler"

   d. "Just Dropped In"

10. When did The First Edition break up?

    a. 1985

    b. 1976

    c. 1973

    d. 1969

11. At the start of his solo career, Kenny Rogers signed a record deal with Columbia Records.

a. True

b. False

12. Kenny Rogers's "Laura" was his first commercial failure.

a. True

b. False

13. Which single did Kenny Rogers release in 1977, immediately after his second solo album?

a. "Runaway Girl"

b. "Lucille"

c. "Laura"

d. "The Gambler"

14. Which song from Kenny Rogers's first solo album was featured in the movie *Trackdown*?

a. "Your Cheating Heart"

b. "Runaway Girl"

c. "Laura"

d. "Love Lifted Me"

15. Who was the producer behind Kenny Rogers's first solo albums?

a. Sam Phillips

b. Webb Pierce

c. Larry Butler

d. Phil Spector

16. Lionel Richie was co-producer for Kenny Rogers's "The Gambler."

a. True

b. False

17. Which of the following songs was written by Bee Gees and performed by Kenny Rogers?

    a. "Lucille"

    b. "Laura"

    c. "Islands in the Stream"

    d. "The Gambler"

18. Some tracks for "We Are the World" were recorded at Kenny Rogers's LA studio in the 80s.

    a. True

    b. False

19. When was Kenny Rogers's album *The Gambler* released?

    a. 1993

    b. 1980

    c. 1976

    d. 1978

20. Kenny Rogers played bass and sang lead vocals for The First Edition's "Just Dropped In."

    a. True

    b. False

QUIZ ANSWER KEY

1. "That Crazy Feeling"

2. False

3. Bobby Doyle Three

4. "Here's That Rainy Day"

5. New Christy Minstrels

6. True

7. False

8. Eddy Arnold

9. "Just Dropped In"

10. 1976

11. False

12. True

13. "Lucille"

14. "Runaway Girl"

15. Larry Butler

16. False

17. "Islands in the Stream"

18. True

19. 1978

20. True

CONCLUSION

As you can see, country music never converged to a single notion; but nor did America itself. This is probably what makes this genre so distinguishable. It has been attacked by cash-hungry accountants and politicians, but in the end, no one was able to delete it.

Whether today's kids can understand country or not depends on many factors. Someone might discover country at a certain age or after a certain event in their life. In any case, there always comes a time for country—the place where all big goals, politics, and talking heads disappear.

One thing is guaranteed, though. Having read this book, you will never listen to country music the same way. The history of the mountain song, the honky tonk, and the cowboy will stick in your mind forever—hopefully. And you will surely nail those trivia games!

Going back to the beginning, we recommended that you try driving on a long a highway and listening to country. Well, now is the best time. Specifically, we recommend "Honky Tonk Heroes (Like Me)" by Waylon Jennings.

Also, listen closely to the soundtracks of the most famous movies. There is a lot of country there, and you already know a lot about it. Not to mention going to a country concert. Luckily, many country legends are still alive; although many have also passed away in recent years.

Finally, if kids call you a redneck for listening to country, don't take it too seriously. As you have seen in this book, the notion of country being redneck music is quite mistaken. This notion was possibly artificially introduced as a part of a political agenda—something very common in America. And those early rock and rollers... Boy, did they copy from country! At least they admit it, though. Listen to what you like, and rest assured that the real stuff cannot get beaten by ill intentions. And if you can pass this stuff on to the next generation, kudos to you!

By the way, Dolly Parton wrote "Coat of Many Colors" at the back of a tour bus, while she was at *the Porter Wagoner Show*. It's a brutally honest song that's definitely worth a listen to start you on your country journey or just to relive a classic. After all, America is the place where you can start off with a ragged coat and become Dolly Parton.

DON'T FORGET YOUR
FREE BOOKS

GET THEM FOR FREE ON WWW.TRIVIABILL.COM

MORE BOOKS BY BILL O'NEILL

I hope you enjoyed this book and learned something new. Please feel free to check out some of my previous books on Amazon.

Made in the USA
Las Vegas, NV
29 October 2021

33324618R00089